# KINGDOM DISCIPLESHIP

## Doing The Lord's Business Until He Comes

### STAN BELYSHEV

# KINGDOM DISCIPLESHIP

## Doing The Lord's Business Until He Comes

StanBelyshev.com



Paperback ISBN: 9798864748343
Kindle ASIN: B0CLBYZFMK
Hardcover ISBN: 9798864807019
Library of Congress Control Number:  2023920073

# CONTENTS

# INTRODUCTION

What exactly is kingdom discipleship? Kingdom discipleship is not simply attending weekly church gatherings, or being a good Christian, or merely reading your Bible and being consistent in your prayer life, or hiding behind your good works, but rather demonstrating and exemplifying Christ in you and Christ through everything you do.

When Jesus walked on this earth, His sole purpose and mission was not to focus on Himself, but rather on the needs of others as He faithfully fulfilled His Father's will, as He once boldly stated to His earthly parents, "Why did you seek Me? Did you not know that I must be about My Father's business?"[1]

What did Jesus mean as a teenager when He said, "I must be about My Father's business?" Even in His early years, He clearly understood His Father's perfect will for His life, and this same perfect will and mindset must be in every heart and mind of those who are born-again and profess that Jesus Christ is their Lord and Savior.

I started writing this book in the summer of 2019 and planned to publish it in late spring of 2020, but in March of that year, the entire world went into a catastrophic tailspin, and throughout that year, much chaos occurred in America with political shifts, protests, shootings, and the list goes on. And because of this tumultuous turbulence, I felt compelled to put the book on hold and wait to see what the body of

Christ would accomplish throughout the speechless 2020 year and the head-spinning 2021 year.

Yes, Christianity and our faith in Jesus Christ are under attack like never before, and our Judeo-Christian nation, America, is collapsing at an alarming rate. The more I think about this tragic circumstance, the more I realize that we can blame the world, blame politicians, blame immorality, blame LGBTQ people, or even blame anything else. The truth is that we, as Christians, are the most obvious problem, and we must take this issue very seriously.

I had a period in my early years as a believer when I was still a green spiritual tomato where I became an expert at playing the Blame Game, but my heavenly Father pulled me back into spiritual alignment with the grace of God, plenty of prayers, and by surrounding myself with kingdom believers. And it is my heart's desire to focus on kingdom discipleship throughout the pages of this book.

Why is discipleship so important? Discipleship is a foundation that every born-again Christian needs. Without it, we are simply constructing our faith on shifting sand. The word disciple or disciples appears or is mentioned more than 270 times in the New Testament. And with such a thought-provoking book title, some of you may be scratching your heads, wondering what the main point of this entire book is. I suppose it's fair to say that my approach is more equivalent to a watchman on the wall rather than from a pastoral, evangelistic, apostolic, or doomsday preacher perspective.

As you dive through the pages of this book, you will be refreshed, encouraged, lovingly slapped with a reality check, and most importantly stirred up with much conviction to re-evaluate your heart and your kingdom purpose on this earth by asking yourself, "Am I a kingdom ambassador or just and average churchgoer?" And am I raising radical and transformational disciples who will become agents of change, as they will bring kingdom influence into their local communities, into academia, into their families and marriages, into social media, into their workplaces, and their spheres of influence?

As you embark on this daring journey through the pages of this book you will be challenged to look at Christianity and your kingdom assignment from a whole different perspective. With everything that has been occurring in our country, in politics, in academia, in media, and in the body of Christ, we have witnessed a drastic spiritual shift. In what way? We are witnessing prominent pastors and influential leaders who speak boldly against racism, social injustice, or equal opportunity, while these same individuals stay silent on abortion, politics and policies, destructive curriculums and liberal professors, socialism, and the vast brainwashing that is spewing through social media and Hollywood.

After witnessing such drastic differences, I became discouraged and even sidetracked at one point, but by the grace of God, I came to the realization that the Holy Spirit is causing a major spiritual shift in America and the body of Christ. We are not entering a period in which it will no longer be about large churches, prominent pastors, influential Christian leaders, New York Times best-selling authors, or those with a large social media following. No, the Lord is raising a nameless generation who are branded by the fire of the Holy Spirit rather than by Christianese culture. Our heavenly Father will transform shepherd David's into giant slayers and kings. He will use nameless people, such as the young Jewish girl who the Lord used to bring healing to her master Naaman, or the nameless woman at the well who brought her entire village to Jesus after her first encounter with the Messiah. And our heavenly Father will be releasing people who have been branded with fire, such as the three Hebrew friends who were thrown into the fiery furnace. And this gives me great hope that our heavenly Father's purpose and agenda are not hampered or limited by our theological, denominational, or traditional practices.

Please do not misinterpret my genuine affection for someone who is frustrated and critical of the body of Christ as you read this book. Also, keep in mind that eight of the twenty-one chapters in this book are accompanied by a question mark. We were all taught at some point in our lives that asking questions is essential for personal growth, and it is my heart's desire to challenge you, my friend, through these vital questions as they relate to your faith, your kingdom purpose on this earth, and the function of your local church.

I have to be honest with you: the examples, illustrations, and language that I utilize in this book are not for the fainthearted. They may provoke you or awaken your spirit man. My friend, if you are ready to roll up your spiritual sleeves and get busy doing the Lord's business until He comes, then I want to encourage you to be willing to pay the necessary price though your kingdom assignment and purpose as you faithfully and wholeheartedly serve and disciple others. The journey may be tough, but its well worth it.

> *"Are people drawn to you because of who you are or because of who you are in Christ?"*

# CHAPTER 1
# DOING THE LORD'S BUSINESS UNTIL HE COMES

When it comes to business, doing business, or owning a business, we all have a good idea of what that entails and what it takes to run a successful and profitable enterprise, but have you ever considered the kingdom of God and the kingdom mandate as a business? Have you ever considered that God's kingdom is similar to a business? And, no, I'm not talking about exploiting the Gospel or using your gifts for the sole purpose of profit, but rather about understanding that the kingdom of God must function as a legitimate business, but not according to man-made principles, standards, or limitations.

Doing the Lord's business until He returns is simply being a good steward of what has been given and entrusted to you, which is your gift of salvation, your kingdom calling and assignment, and, most importantly, your time on this earth. Furthermore, as we see in the gospels, the master bestowed different talents (kingdom assignments) on three of his servants to see what they would do with them, with two increasing their talents and one hiding his talent. And in like manner it is entirely up to us whether we use and develop our kingdom talent(s) or hide them behind our numerous excuses, which we frequently construct out of self-pity or selfishness.

Building the Lord's kingdom business shares many similarities and principles with regular business, where the success of that business determines the income and longevity, but most businesses fail within their first two to three years. This divine principle also applies to kingdom discipleship, as many churches struggle, have a high turnover rate, or eventually close their doors because raising and developing mature disciples of Christ was not a priority or was highly neglected.

So, the concept and mandate of kingdom discipleship is for God's children to focus our heart and spirit man on doing the Lord's business until He returns for His bride. Even Tony Evans once said this insightful statement, "We've got to move from membership to discipleship to being full-time Christians, not part-time saints."[1] Wow!

I once heard a Christian parable that went something like this:

*A long time ago a Christian missionary came to a native Indian village and with the sincerity of his heart he preached and evangelized to the whole village for hours. At the end of his genuine preaching, he turned to Chief Blackhawk and said, "Hey Chief Blackhawk, what did you think about my sermon and its content?" The chief looked at him and replied, "Preacher, you spoke like much thunder and lightning, but you never provided the rain!"*

The irony of this story is that you can act, talk, behave, and be very knowledgeable as a Christian, but your life will be devoid of fruit or substance. This highlights the problem with Christians and Christianity, where we and our faith often appear pathetic. And in this chapter, I want to draw your attention to whether your heart is completely committed to serving the Lord and whether your faith is pathetic or proactive.



## YOU ARE EITHER 100% IN OR 100% OUT

How many of you want to drive halfway to your vacation destination? Or get halfway married? Or fall in love halfway? Or get your car fixed halfway? Or get half of your paycheck? I don't see any of you waving your hands! I don't see anyone waving their hands! Why should it be any different when it comes to us fully committing our lives to the Lord and His kingdom assignment for us here on earth?

You are either 100 hundred percent in or 100 hundred percent out! There is no such thing as a middle ground or doing it halfway. Jesus did not die halfway! We did not receive half of the Bible! The Holy Spirit did not partially manifest into your heart! And most importantly you are not halfway saved by the blood of Jesus Christ. Hello! As a child of God, we need to honestly evaluate the gospel message and what Jesus firmly declared, Then He said to *them* all, "If anyone desires to come after Me, let him deny himself, and take up his cross daily, and follow Me."[2]

*Deny* and *daily* are the two keywords in the preceding verse. As Jesus' followers, we must deny ourselves, which means putting aside our desires and ambitions and committing ourselves completely to the Lord. We must also take up the cross on a daily basis, which requires complete surrender to God's will. This means that we are either a true disciple of Jesus Christ or a typical churchgoer who exhibits outward lip service.

> *"To be a true disciple of Christ, you must fully commit and surrender to His will and His Word."*

## CRAPPY LIFE OR SPIRITUAL MANURE?

I'm guilty of complaining a lot about my life and the things I've had to endure, which has led to the publication of my second book, *When Life Is Full of It*. One of the most common misunderstandings among born-again Christians, in my opinion, is that we misinterpret God's spiritual manure for the crap (pardon my bluntness) that happens in our lives. No one is immune to adversity, trials, problems, or tragic events, but all of this is merely spiritual manure that our heavenly Father is incorporating into our lives so that we can spiritually grow and mature and eventually produce much fruit for His kingdom.

If we carefully examine the entire Bible, we will notice endless patterns of how God's children and Biblical personas had to endure many hardships, persecution, pain, and opposition, which appeared to be the wrong end of the stick, not realizing that it was the Lord who was pouring His spiritual manure around them, so they would be fruitful and bear much fruit for the kingdom of God. And even the Apostle Paul used these words to remind and encourage young Timothy, "You therefore must endure hardship as a good soldier of Jesus Christ."[3]

So, my friend, the next time you selfishly begin to feel as if all of the crap in your life is being poured on purpose, begin to assess these moments through the living Word of God, which will show you a whole different perspective where your heavenly Father is simply pruning your branches and fertilizing your faith so you can become stronger, more mature, and greatly influential on this earth.

We would simply be a bunch of religious people full of legalism, bitterness, and theological error if we didn't have this spiritual manure in our lives. And here's something to think about! Have your beliefs, ideology, theology, and traditions drawn people closer or further away from Jesus? And, do people look forward to seeing you, or do they try to avoid you? This was merely a reality check questionnaire!

The truth is that God's spiritual manure frequently comes from His living Word, as His Word begins to fertilize our inner spirit man, producing much fruit for His kingdom. However, if we are not bearing kingdom fruit, those around us will only see and taste man-made theology, traditions, and religiosity. My challenge to you my friend is to be a true follower of Jesus, as you allow the Holy Spirit to continue to fertilize your heart, your mind, and your spirit man.

> **"A religious person will identify as a Baptist, Catholic, Charismatic, Methodist, or Pentecostal, whereas a child of God will identify as a follower of Jesus Christ."**

## ARE YOU A PATHETIC OR A PROACTIVE CHRISTIAN?

It is a personal choice to be unhappy or pitiful. And being a person of dedication and passion, on the other hand, is also a personal choice. And openly reevaluating whether you and I are pathetic or proactive Christians is not a question of insult or rebuke, but of honestly analyzing our hearts on whether we are genuine disciples of Jesus Christ or whether I'm just a dumb sheep that are part of the herd going in whatever direction the other sheep are going.

To be the disciple that Jesus desires, or at least what the Word of God defines as true discipleship, we must return to the original source, His living Word, and the counselor and teacher of our soul, the Holy Spirit. The Bible is the ultimate truth, and the Holy Spirit will reveal it to us all and show us God's perfect will for our lives, as well as keep us on the path of righteousness.

As the world, our culture, and society continue to shift in the wrong direction, keep in mind that God's Word and His commandments never change. And as others begin to tell you and me that we must conform to the relevance of our modern time, the Bible reminds us, "And do not be conformed to this world, but be transformed by the renewing of your mind, that you may prove what *is* that good and acceptable and perfect will of God."[4]

Apathy indicates that your spirit man and heart have become cold or lukewarm. And this is a very dangerous spiritual condition to be in, especially in these last days. We are living in a prophetic time where our heavenly Father will do marvelous things through the power of the Holy Spirit like never before, and we as His children must position our heart, mind, and inner spirit man in a proactive posture. And as we align ourselves with God's perfect will, we give the Holy Spirit the necessary permission to use us as tools for building and establishing God's kingdom on this earth. So, my brother and sister in Christ, I challenge you to be a proactive Christian rather than a pathetic one.

> *"How many people will be better off because of who you are and what value and worth you can add to their life."*

# CHAPTER 2
# ARE WE BABYSITTING OR MAKING DISCIPLES?

I had my fair share of babysitting someone else's child and plenty of years raising my own three. Babysitting serves a specific purpose, function, and result. But what happens when the same babysitting model is applied to discipleship? Allow me to amuse you:

**Babysitting**

**+**

**Discipleship**

**=**

*Spiritually Immature Christians*

The book of Hebrews has a powerful proclamation as it relates to discipleship: "You have been believers so long now that you ought to be teaching others. Instead, you need someone to teach you again the basic things about God's word. You are like babies who need milk and cannot eat solid food. For someone who lives on milk is still an infant and doesn't know how to do what is right. Solid food is for those who are mature, who through training have the skill to recognize the difference between right and wrong."[1]

I would not be exaggerating if I said that many churches and church programs have devolved into social clubs or social events where we focus on pampering one another rather than equipping one another. This became clear in the story of the Israelites as they wandered for forty years in the wilderness. And Moses had a multi-million-member congregation at the time, and the moaning, groaning and complaining never stopped. It got so bad at times that God had to pull out His heavenly belt and discipline their spiritual butt-cheeks, which resulted in the deaths of thousands. And as you progress through this chapter, you will be compelled to answer the following question: "Am I babysitting or making disciples?"

> *"True discipleship is when you can bring the sheep to the green pastures and still waters, not when you build a bigger sheep-pen."*

## IT'S TIME TO GROW UP!

When my teenage son gets out of line by mouthing off to me or my wife, I usually tell him, "Hey, these same hands that held you when you were a baby will become the same hands that will smack you on the head!" And my son would usually respond, "Sorry, papa!" I don't say these things to threaten my son; rather, I say them to emphasize that he has no right to treat his father or, especially, his mother with such disrespect.

What is the takeaway here? When my son was a baby, I could only talk to or discipline him in ways that were appropriate or proportional to his understanding. But now that he's a seventeen-year-old with raging hormones, I have to take my disciplinary actions to a whole new level. This is a spiritual core principle! We are spiritual babies when we first come to the Lord, but we must grow out of that stage and become mature disciples of Christ. The tragic issue with many Christians is that they do not grow past the infancy stage and continue to moan and groan like babies for the rest of their Christian lives. Or even worse, they drift away and revert to their former sinful ways.

Having served as a youth pastor for ten years gave me the privilege of witnessing how many young lives were transformed over those years, and I still see what God is doing in their lives, families, marriages, and kingdom purpose through their social media posts today. On the other hand, I have seen certain youth who were like an unsettled wave in the sea, tossed back and forth, and it breaks my heart to see those same individuals struggling with the same sinful lifestyles or those who have fallen away from their walk with the Lord even today.

I wholeheartedly believe that our heavenly Father has more grace and patience for His children than we can imagine, but He is also not naive and will use whatever means necessary for His children to mature spiritually. And this is frequently accomplished through disciplinary actions, which are always unsettling for anyone. And, just as any earthly parent desires to see their child fully mature, our heavenly

Father desires to see us all fully mature through His Son Jesus, which is why we all need to grow up.

> *"Spiritual growth and maturity do not occur solely as a result of Bible study. It is the result of our daily decision to allow the Holy Spirit to change and transform us."*

## BABY POWDER OR THE POWER OF THE HOLY SPIRIT?

During the infancy of all three of my children, I would frequently notice my wife kissing their silky butt cheeks after a bath or even a diaper change. I'm sure my wife isn't the only passionate mother who did something like this, but you can't blame her because those baby butt cheeks are soft, gentle, and fluffy. In addition, if the baby had a typical rash, we would apply cream or baby powder to relieve the burn or discomfort. Now that my children are older, I don't recall my wife doing the same thing, because that season has passed and my children are no longer infants.

With that said, if the local church focuses on spiritually powdering and pampering new believers or even seasoned Christians, we shouldn't be surprised that many still have immature faith or will soon fall away from walking with the Lord. One crucial aspect that is missing is the power of the Holy Spirit, which has the ability to change and transform the hearts and minds of every child of God. This isn't anything new, but it's still a critical missing link.

Even Apostle Paul reminded the Thessalonians with these words, "For our gospel did not come to you in word only, but also in power, and in the Holy Spirit and in much assurance, as you know what kind of men we were among you for your sake."[2] And if we only speak good words but do not operate in the power of the Holy Spirit, we are only offering spiritual baby powder to one another, which will keep many as spiritually immature children of God, whereas the Word of God challenges us to function and operate in the power of the Holy Spirit, which will form true kingdom disciples. And true kingdom discipleship is like a bricklayer who constructs a house out of bricks that can withstand all of life's storms. Therefore, the body of Christ must raise bricklayers rather than straw pickers!

> *"The true essence of discipleship is when you teach every believer about all of the blessings and promises we have in Christ, as well as all of the challenges, struggles, and suffering you will face in your daily walk with the Lord."*

## THE COST OF DISCIPLESHIP

Being a disciple of Christ is not a free membership. Yes, salvation is a free gift from God, even though it cost Jesus His life, but becoming and remaining a disciple of Jesus has a cost. This is confirmed by the gospel of Luke, which states, "You cannot be my disciple, unless you love me more than you love your father and mother, your wife and children, and your brothers and sisters. You cannot come with me unless you love me more than you love your own life. You cannot be my disciple unless you carry your own cross and come with me."[3]

I'm sure we've all decided to save money by purchasing something much cheaper, despite the fact that there was a good chance that whatever we were buying wasn't of the highest quality. And I'm confident that, despite having an inner gut feeling that we might later regret purchasing at a lower price, we ignored that feeling and went ahead with our original decision. And as time passed, we realized that our initial decision was incorrect, but we were too focused on saving a lot of money to benefit us in the short term.

You see, as Christians, we have a bad habit of trying to take shortcuts or not being willing to pay the price of being a true disciple of Jesus. And for a short time, everything appears to be fine, until we are confronted with personal difficulties, family issues, or various illnesses. And it is often during these trying times that many Christians become spiritually broken, angry at God, and even abandon their faith. As a result, paying the price for being a true disciple of Jesus is something you and I will have to do for as long as we have breath in our nostrils.

Furthermore, there must be a sharp distinction between God's children and the children of this world, or, as John put it, "the children of the devil." With so much cohabitation currently taking place, it is difficult to distinguish between those who are genuine followers of Christ and those who simply call themselves Christians.

However, Jesus sternly addressed the distinction between those who are "hot," "cold," and "lukewarm": "So then, because you are lukewarm, and neither cold nor hot, I will vomit you out of my mouth."[4] And these are not words to be taken lightly, as they are a stern warning to those who call themselves followers of Christ. We live in a time when Jesus will use His sword to separate, expose, and cut off the lukewarm, leaving only those who are truly desiring to pay the kingdom cost of being a true follower and disciple of Jesus.

> **"If you call yourself a disciple of Jesus but don't change, and nothing or no one around you changes, then you're just a regular churchgoer."**

## CONVERTING DAYCARES INTO MILITARY BOOT CAMPS

If we truly want to be honest here, we can't deny that our local churches are teeming with soft and tender believers, and I don't mean in terms of their hearts, but of their spiritual maturity and stamina. One solution is to transform our modern-day spiritual daycares into military boot camps, with the Holy Spirit as the drill sergeant and the Word of God as the commandments that strengthen the inner spiritual man.

One of the greatest spiritual drill sergeants, Apostle Paul, had this advice for new believers when he said, "When I was a child, I talked like a child, I thought like a child, I reasoned like a child. When I became a man, I put the ways of childhood behind me."[5] Just as every individual goes through a natural growth process from infancy to childhood, to youth, to adulthood, so does our spiritual growth, and Apostle Paul gives us all sound insight that there will come a time when we must put our childhood behind us and become a spiritually mature child of God and a strong military-like disciple of Jesus who does not need to be constantly pampered.

I wholeheartedly believe and know that the body of Christ contains a large number of believers who are allowing the Holy Spirit and the living Word of God to shape them into strong warriors of Christ who are and will usher in kingdom influence in their town, city, state, and nation. However, this should not be limited to those few but should be a standard for every born-again believer and every local church. The time has come to stop babysitting and start making disciples who are willing to pay the price, willing to walk and fulfill their kingdom calling, and willing to be used as tools in God's Almighty hands on this earth.

> *"One of the primary missions of the local church is to establish God's kingdom on earth, not to form babysitter clubs where we pamper each other with seeker-sensitive theology."*

# CHAPTER 3
# WHAT IS MY CHURCH DOING?

Every local church and ministry are unique, and they all serve a specific purpose and fulfill a kingdom assignment on this earth. Having said that, they cannot stray from the biblical fundamentals that have already been outlined in the Word of God, no matter how much they may focus on their local community or their specific functionality. And as you progress through this chapter, you will be asked, "What is my church doing?" And I'm not talking about the programs or church events, or even your influence in the community; I'm talking about whether your local church is in alignment with the Word of God as it relates to every precious soul who is a current member or a regular attendee.

> *"Are you raising and disciplining others into your image (Adventist, Baptist, Catholic, Charismatic, Methodist, Pentecostal), or into the image of Christ?"*

## CAN GOD REALLY USE THEM?

I was zealous for the Lord and full of self-righteousness in my early years as a green and unripe spiritual tomato. And when

I became a youth pastor, I brought many of those legalistic beliefs with me. For example, I would notice how certain youth or members of the church would frequently return to the altar to repent or give their lives to the Lord. And as I watched them, I became judgmental and critical, wondering why they kept repenting and giving their lives to the Lord on a regular basis.

After ten years of serving as a youth pastor, I can humbly say that I'm grateful that the person I was in my early years of ministry was not the same person I was in later years. God's grace is truly amazing. Anyway, it was difficult for me to see kingdom potential or the God-given gift or abilities that some youth possessed in those early years of ministry. Why? Because I was looking at them through the lenses of my self-righteousness and legalistic thinking!

I guess I was constantly asking myself, "Can God really use this kind of person?" He certainly can! Now, I'm not naive to the notion that we should allow any and every novice or one-day-old born-again person to jump into ministry, but I do want to emphasize the importance of not cutting off any individual who is still trying to get closer to the Lord or grow stronger in their faith, even if they frequently fall or stumble in the process.

Jesus once challenged the religious leaders of His time when they zealously desired to stone an adulterous woman. And here one of the powerful lessons is that we all come from a background that was full of garbage and sinfulness, but no matter how horrible our previous life was, we still have unfathomable hope through the blood and the forgiveness of Jesus.

Let us take a closer look at some of the biblical personas with a shady past whom the Lord did not abandon, but used powerfully when they submitted to His perfect will:

- *Rahab* was a prostitute!
- *Samson* was a womanizer!
- *King David* committed adultery!
- *Apostle Thomas* was a doubter!
- *King Solomon* had too many girlfriends!
- *Saul (Apostle Paul)* persecuted Christians!
- *Apostle Peter* had a big mouth and denied Christ three times!
- *Matthew* was a despised tax collector!
- *The Woman at The Well* had 5 husbands and was currently living with her boyfriend!

So, what's your justification for not allowing the Lord to use you? Or, alternatively, what justifiable reason can you think of to limit or restrict any person from fulfilling their kingdom purpose on this earth? Yes, God has the ability and desire to use every living human being to further His greater purpose on this planet. However, His desire is limited by either the individual's sinful lifestyle or an unrepented heart, or by those within the body of Christ who are operating through judgmentalism and are not seeing the kingdom potential that a particular person possesses.

And because of this, many people have become victims of religious, theological, or dogmatic ideologies within their local church that have restricted or blocked certain people from trying to function or operate in their calling, simply because their previous life before receiving Christ was visible to many. This was also true in my case, as some people who knew me as a rebellious sinner found it difficult to accept me as a child of God who possessed a great purpose.

Again, if God took a murderer like Saul and by His grace transformed him into one of the most historically influential kingdom ambassadors, then God can also take the worst sinners of all and make them into one of the greatest gospel preachers in our modern-day culture. Whether you are a pastor, a church member, a newly born-again believer, or a passionate follower of Jesus, you must seriously ponder on the question, "What is my church doing to advance the kingdom mandate on this earth?"

> *"Successful kingdom leaders are those who have taught and trained others to talk; to think; to walk; to behave, and to influence like Jesus."*

## THE GOSPEL OF CONDEMNATION OR RECONCILIATION?

It is almost instinctive for us to say something negative or to look down on someone. Why? Because, despite being born-again, our fallen Adamic nature is corrupt and always in need of God's grace and mercy. And as born-again Christians, we are still full of selfishness, carnality, and a slew of other flaws that none of us want to discuss. As a result, we sometimes fail to notice how quickly we can position our hearts to condemn another person because of their sin or weaknesses, rather than attempting to position our hearts and spirit man in assisting that other individual to reconcile with the lover of their soul.

It is easy to condemn someone, which we often do out of self-righteousness, but it is difficult to position ourselves as servants whom the Holy Spirit can use to bring another soul into reconciliation with their Creator. This necessitates humility, selflessness, and, above all, love. Take a moment now to examine your heart to determine whether you are preaching the gospel of condemnation or the gospel of reconciliation.

### *What is the gospel of Condemnation?*
- Legalism
- Self-Righteousness
- Religion
- The Pharisee spirit
- Judgementalism
- Criticism

### *What is the gospel of Reconciliation?*
- Grace
- Forgiveness
- Redemption
- Care and Servanthood
- Love, Love, and Love

## HELLO! ONE BODY BUT MANY MEMBERS

Have you ever heard statements like these? This is my church! I'm the leader here! I'm in charge! When you are the pastor then you can do whatever, you like! This is how we have always done this! If you don't like it, then leave!

The epistle of Romans and First Corinthians powerfully stress the point that we have one body, but many members that are supposed to come into unity for one kingdom purpose:

*For as we have many members in one body, but all the members do not have the same function, so we, being many, are one body in Christ, and individually members of one body.* (Romans 12:4-5)

And Apostle Paul once more broadens his point:

*For as the body is one and has many members, but all the members of that one body, so also is Christ.* (1 Corinthians 12:12)

If a local church chooses to ignore this divine directive, it will create an authoritative and legalistic atmosphere, causing the sheep to scatter. In those same passages, it is stated that each member (individual) has a specific purpose, function, and spiritual gift that differs from their fellow believer and that the whole body is edified only when each member comes together in unity. However, when there is no unity, the body malfunctions, resulting in church splits, divisions, hatred, and a myriad of confused, irritated, and lost sheep.

Again, the sole purpose of any local church is to assist each child of God in discovering and comprehending their kingdom identity and purpose, which is accomplished through discipleship. Yes, no church is perfect, and there is no such thing as a perfect pastor or a congregation of super holy and sanctified members. Such churches do not exist, but what does exist is our heavenly Father's desire for His children to dwell in unity and love, while also positioning their hearts in service to others, as we have great compassion for the lost and brokenhearted.

> *"We are commanded to make disciples after the likeness of Christ, not after the likeness of your denomination, theology, or man-made doctrines."*

# CHAPTER 4
# POLITICAL CORRECTNESS VS THE TRUTH

The world and society are changing, and you should be as well! This appears to be a very popular statement, as we frequently hear it in the news media, academia, and on various social media platforms. So, what exactly is the essence and declaration of the preceding statement? It is fairly straightforward! Your old school, your beliefs are out of date, you need to be more relevant, or your point of view is outdated! Everything is changing, and you need to get on board!

I'm all for relevance! I believe that God creates everything new! I'm also open to new ideas! But at what price? It is not surprising that churches around the world have changed their approaches to evangelism, outreach, church programs, and discipleship training. This is all wonderful, but at what cost? And in this nail-biting chapter, I will challenge you to spiritually discern and honestly re-examine your heart in relation to the truth of God's Word and much of the worldly nonsense that has crept into our local churches. Even Jesus had a rebuke towards the multitudes that followed Him, when He said, "Hypocrites! You can discern the face of the sky and of the earth, but how *is it* you do not discern this time?"[1]

## LEGALISM vs A LEGAL DOCUMENT

We have a plethora of legal documents in our society that are intended to protect you or make you aware of your personal rights. Some people use these legal documents to defend their rights or causes, while others may use similar documents against you in court. And, to no one's surprise, Christianity and fellow believers have been in a constant tug of war when it comes to legalism or the truths written in God's Word. And here, I want to emphasize the Word of God as a legal kingdom document rather than a legalistic book of rules.

Let's get right to some contentious issues that many Christians wrestle with or have endless debates about. Here are a couple of examples: Is the practice or lifestyle of homosexuality a sin, or did God create them that way? Is it possible that when someone decides to change their gender, God made a mistake while forming that person in their mother's womb? So, what about abortion? Is there any authoritative insight in the Bible on this critical issue, or are we free to make our own decisions? What about sin? Do we have the authority to choose what the Bible says about sin or specific sinful lifestyles?

It's truly amazing how attorneys on both sides try to use or manipulate the definition of a specific law in their client's favor in a court of law. This is not a new phenomenon, but many criminals have been released and many innocent people have been indicted. So it should come as no surprise that legal documents or laws can be twisted or misinterpreted, but when we take the living Word of God, which is a legal kingdom document, and try to twist or interpret it to our benefit or our sinful lifestyle, we have a serious problem on our hands.

Yes, there are plenty of legalistic Christians, but I want to focus solely on those who claim to be born-again believers but refuse to hear the whole truth, or those who pick and choose from the Bible to what seems convenient, or those who refuse to hear anything that contradicts their sinful lifestyle.

No matter how we twist, turn, or interpret the Bible while we are still alive on earth, at the end of our lives, you and I will stand before the righteous Judge, and He will judge us in accordance with the original legal document that He presented to all of humanity, and all of our arguments, justifications and theological beliefs will be rendered null and void in God's court of law. And this same legal document has a sober reminder for all, as it once stated, "Therefore God also has highly exalted Him and given Him the name which is above every name, that at the name of Jesus every knee should bow, of those in heaven, and of those on earth, and of those under this earth, and *that* every tongue should confess that Jesus Christ *is* Lord, to the glory of God the Father."[2] It makes no difference who you are or what you believe or do not believe, but there will come a time when all of humanity will fully acknowledge and comprehend that Jesus is the Son of God and that His legal document (Bible) is the only truth.

*"When people are around you, do they see the reflection of Jesus or the reflection of your denomination, ideology, and religiosity?"*

## POLITICAL CORRECTNESS OR THE TRUTH?

The term political correctness is defined as a belief that one has that language and actions that could be offensive to others.[3] So, how then do you reconcile what is the truth, with political correctness? As we glance at the scriptures, we read the words of Jesus, Then Jesus said to them, "If you abide in My word, you are my disciples indeed. And you shall know the truth, and the truth shall make you free."[4]

I've been very active on social media in the areas of discipleship, personal development (via coaching and mentoring), and politics. It gives me great inner fulfillment to be able to release my kingdom potential in these spheres. I could only imagine Apostle Paul fully utilizing the remarkable platform of social media. But, as someone who has spent a lot of time on this platform, I've come across a lot of confused people, a lot of garbage, a lot of nonsense, and a lot of theologically twisted beliefs. And, yes, I'm referring to all of the above regarding those who identify as Christians.

I could respect people's personal theological beliefs or revelations because we are all limited to some extent by our understanding or interpretation of God's Word. But when the Bible says something in plain and clear language and then you start twisting it to your convenience or liking, you've crossed a dangerous line. Many Christians, particularly among the younger generation, support abortion, the LGBTQ lifestyle, same-sex marriage, and even gender change. And there are those who claim that this person was born this way because God created them that way, frequently referring to those who live a homosexual lifestyle. If all of the above is true, then we as Christians have a serious problem. And this is about the Bible's integrity and credibility, which is the truth. Either what we read is true or it isn't. There is no such thing as a middle ground!

We begin to jeopardize the truth of God's Word when we introduce political correctness into the body of Christ or our Christian faith. And when we begin to jeopardize the truth of God's Word, we disregard or dismiss what the Bible is attempting to teach or warn us about that particular belief, lifestyle, or behavior. When Jesus stood before Pontius Pilate during His trial, Pilate had a crucial conversation with Him in which Jesus told him, "Everyone who is of the truth hears My voice. Pilate said to Him, "What is truth?' And when he had said this, he went out again to the Jews."[5]

The takeaway lesson here is that Pilate was on the right track when he tried to question Jesus about the truth, but the problem was that he never gave Jesus the opportunity to tell him about this truth. This is exactly what is happening in the body of Christ and among many Christian people who presumably love the Lord, attend church, and even read the Bible, but have not allowed the *logos* of the Word to become a *rhema* in their spirit man, and as a result, many have become either legalistic or deaf to the truth of God's Word. As a result, many so-called Christians are no longer aligning their faith or walk with the Lord in accordance with His truth. As a result, there is much confusion and division among many Christians, with those who choose to abide or believe what the Bible says are being labeled as religious bigots or irrelevant believers by their fellow Christians who disregard the integrity or origin of God's Word.

Yes, you have every right to be politically correct so that you do not offend those who live in opposition to the truth of God's Word, but by doing so, you are straying away from the truth that is supposed to set you free and set others free from any worldly bondage. And, once again, I challenge you to align your heart and spirit man with living truth rather than worldly political correctness.

> *"Our heavenly Father did not command us to share our personal opinions with others, but to share the Good News gospel."*

## DID NOT JESUS COMMAND US TO LOVE EVERYONE?

Is it true that Jesus commanded us to love everyone? He did, indeed! True and genuine Godly love, on the other hand, is derived from the truth, and that truth is founded on the living Word of God. We love everyone, even the worst sinner because the Bible commands us to. However, the Bible also teaches us to speak the truth, even if it is controversial to some and offensive to others, and to righteously judge those who live a sinful lifestyle or disobedience God's Word.

God is love, and love is God. God's love is perfect and divine, but it is not gullible or blind. God's love captivates men's hearts and also penetrates men's hearts. God's love can cover you like a heavenly blanket while also exposing you to the bone. God's love can show us a glimpse of heaven, but it can also show us a glimpse of hell. God's love is not biased or dual-minded because it stems from the truth, and that truth is Jesus.

When you hear the enigmatic phrase, "How could such a loving God allow such tragedy to occur?" You must always take a step back and process such narrow-minded statements or understandings through God's Word. And when you do, you'll realize that such childish statements have no weight but sound appealing to a lot of people. You see, when we confine God to a specific event, deed, tragedy, or situation, we have reduced God to our inadequate earthly limitations and understanding. First, God is not a man with flaws and weaknesses; rather, He is divine, perfect, all-knowing, and all-loving.

And, just as Jesus teaches us to love our neighbor, He also teaches us to speak the truth. However, if we choose to be politically correct in order not to offend someone's feelings, we are distorting the essence of who God is and why

He sent His One and Only Son to die on the cross. The death of Jesus on the cross was a bold statement declaring that we were all sinners condemned to hell, but the love of Christ through His death and resurrection gave us hope and a future, but this truth cannot be presented to a dying world in a politically correct pamphlet.

> *"God's love does not require approval from others, but it does require the heart, mouth, hands, and feet of mankind to make it visible to others."*

# CHAPTER 5
# A PHARISEE OR A CHILD OF GOD?

Pharisee or a God's child? Is this meant to be a trick question? The Pharisees of the New Testament were religious leaders who could be compared to pastors or church leaders today, but in this chapter, I want to focus on the religious mindset and legalistic view that a born-again Christian may have. And it is this particular mindset and heart attitude that has made the body of Christ look dreadful and has left Christianity with a sour taste in the hearts and minds of many.

If you read the gospels carefully, you will see how legalistic, selfish, and religiously insane the Pharisees, Sadducees, and Scribes were. Not only did they have a problem with who Jesus was, but they were also enraged by the fact that He performed supernatural miracles on the Sabbath. They couldn't care less if someone was healed or delivered from demons; all they cared about was that the law of Moses was not broken.

"You can be very heavenly-minded but no earthly good," someone once said. This was an issue with the Pharisees during Jesus' time, and it is still an issue in the body of Christ today. And if you and I truly want to be God's children, we must set aside our legalistic beliefs, theological dogmas, and self-righteousness. And as we progress through this chapter, you will be required to honestly examine your heart to see if there is a Pharisee-type spirit present, as well as grasp the powerful revelation that God is your Father because you are His child.

"You are a child of God because Jesus said so."

## WOE TO YOU

At one point, Jesus had enough of these religious and bigoted Pharisee's where He said:

*"But woe to you, scribes and Pharisees, hypocrites! For you shut up the kingdom of heaven against men; for you neither go in yourselves, nor do you allow those who are entering to go in. Woe to you, scribes and Pharisees, hypocrites! For you devour widows' houses, and for a pretense make long prayers. Therefore you will receive greater condemnation. "Woe to you, scribes and Pharisees, hypocrites! For you travel land and sea to win one proselyte, and when he is won, you make him twice as much a son of hell as yourselves. "Woe to you, blind guides, who say, 'Whoever swears by the temple, it is nothing; but whoever swears by the gold of the temple, he is obliged to perform it.' "Woe to you, scribes and Pharisees, hypocrites! For you cleanse the outside of the cup and dish,*

*but inside they are full of extortion and self-indulgence. "Woe to you, scribes and Pharisees, hypocrites! For you are like whitewashed tombs which indeed appear beautiful outwardly, but inside are full of dead men's bones and all uncleanness.*[1]

I guess the question that you and I need to honestly ask ourselves is: Would Jesus be saying the same thing to us, "Woe to you Stan!" I sincerely hope not! However, the Holy Spirit is always working overtime upon our hearts, which gives us hope and an opportunity to constantly re-evaluate our heart and our mindset to ensure that we are a child of God and not a zealous Pharisee.

> **"Man's self-righteousness appears to be a cute furry skunk on the outside, but on the inside is packed with stinky religion."**

## ARE YOU A TRUE DISCIPLE?

Are you a disciple of Jesus Christ? Are you certain? Again, are you certain? Sorry for the exaggeration, but the above question is meant to be taken seriously, not jokingly. Any building structure, you see, requires a foundation. Before there can be a harvest, the farmer must first sow the seed. Before a child can be born, it must first be conceived and then develop for a nine-month cycle in the mother's womb. In other words, God has orchestrated universal laws and principles that must be in harmony.

In the same way, the question of whether or not you are a true disciple is in accordance with divine laws, which Jesus outlined when He said, "A new commandment I give to you, that you love one another; as I have loved you, that you also love one another. By this all will know that you are My disciples, if you have love for one another."[2] In the body of Christ, the word "love" has been exaggerated and misused. It appears that the word "love" has been used in the same context as it would be used for food, things, hobbies, or other various events. However, we cannot apply Jesus' commandment to love one another in the same way that we love to eat our favorite food. Or our passion for a particular hobby.

The reason for my above outline is that we preach, teach, proclaim, and attempt to declare that the Christian faith is founded on love. And while all of the preceding should be true, a major paradox emerges when we examine the spiritual condition of the body of Christ as a whole. Let us look at some of these paradoxes:

- We are still fighting for our doctrinal beliefs.
- We hide behind our denominational ideologies while pointing out the errors in other denominations.
- We eagerly await the capture or witnessing of a notable man or woman of God going astray or committing a sinful deed.
- We enjoy discussing the sins or weaknesses of our fellow Christ-followers.

- We are unwilling to change our old traditions or programs.
- We are easily offended when the pastor or other fellow Christian's address or point out sinful lifestyles or sinful behaviors.

To be a true disciple of Christ means that you and I need to focus on building the kingdom of God on this earth and not waste our valuable time gossiping about others. It also means that we need to invest our valuable time into fulfilling our kingdom assignment on this earth, without wasting our valuable time arguing or debating theological doctrines or man-made ideologies.

> *"The essence of discipleship is to exemplify Christ in your personal life, not to persuade others about Him."*

## IS GOD MY FATHER?

The revelation that God, the Creator of everything, is our heavenly Father is one of the most misunderstood and even misplaced perceptions of the scriptures. Yes, the Bible is full of references to God as our Father, but it appears that many born-again believers still struggle with this profound insight, and even churches or certain denominations don't place enough emphasis on the fact that the One who created us is also our heavenly Father.

Is God my Father? He is, indeed! So, how can a perfect divine being be referred to as my Father? Or, more specifically, how can an eternal and immortal being have a relationship with a mortal being who has a temporary body and a very short lifespan? This powerful truth will render you speechless and perplexed.

In my early years as a Christian, I had to grasp the divine revelation of God as my Father. It didn't happen right away, but when it did, it changed my entire walk with the Lord, and this breakthrough happened mostly when my first child was born. My son Justin's birth began to transform my entire understanding of God as my heavenly Father. And now that I'm a father, I'm reading the Bible from a whole new perspective. I suppose the honest question is whether it is necessary to bring a child into this world for them to understand that God is their Father. No! This revelation must be personal and never limited to your earthly status or specific accomplishments.

God is your Father because Jesus said so! The New Testament is replete with bold declarations that proceeded through the mouth of Jesus:

*"Let your light so shine before men, that they may see your good works and glorify **your Father** in heaven."* (Matthew 5:16)

*"Therefore you shall be perfect, just as **your Father** in heaven is perfect."* (Matthew 5:48)

*"But you, when you pray, go into your room, and when you have  shut your door,  pray  to **your Father** who is in  the secret place; and **your Father** who sees in secret will reward you openly."* (Matthew 6:6)

*"In this manner, therefore, pray:  **Our Father** in heaven, Hallowed be Your name."* (Matthew 6:9)

*"For if you forgive men their trespasses, **your heavenly Father** will also forgive you."* (Matthew 6:14)

Wow, this is truly incredible! And I honestly believe that one of the primary reasons why many Christians portray or exemplify a Pharisee-like spirit is that they have yet to grasp the truth that God is their Father, and as a result, they are spiritual orphans, and the enemy of our soul frequently victimizes such individuals. But today I want to tell you that you are God's child!

> ***"The day you discover your identity in Christ is the day you realize you are a child of God."***

# CHAPTER 6
# WHERE IS MY REWARD?

**W**hat am I going to get? What is the benefit to me? How much money will I be paid? Is there going to be any sort of reward for this? These are far too common questions, and I'm sure we've all been guilty of asking them at some point in our lives.

Every year, the church we used to attend did community outreach, and one year I told my teenage son that we would be participating. His first response was, "What will I get from this?" And I quickly replied, "Nothing!" with a smirk on my face. I then began to explain to my son that whenever we do a good deed, such as this community outreach, we should never expect a reward here on earth, but rather focus on the reward that awaits us in eternity. This was just another teachable moment between father and son.

I can't get angry or frustrated about my son's original question because he's still learning and growing, but this situation speaks volumes about the heart attitude and mindset of many Christians who are always looking for some kind of reward. Yes, there is a reward, but we do not serve others solely for the purpose of obtaining an earthly reward. And it is my sincere desire to address the attitude of our hearts and the significance of servanthood in this chapter.

## THE HARVEST IS RIPE BUT WHERE ARE THE LABORERS?

As Jesus was going throughout various cities and villages, He had much compassion on the people, which made Him utter this evangelistic statement to His disciples, "The harvest truly *is* plentiful, but the laborers *are* few."[1] This same phrase was repeated behind the pulpits in such religious contexts that it made me spiritually nauseous. Most preachers declare that we must go out into the streets and evangelize, that we must go to Africa on a mission, or that we must tell all of our neighbors about Jesus. That sounds very spiritual in context, but, like many other Bible passages, this verse has been and continues to be butchered.

We often get caught up in the first part of that verse, "The harvest truly is plentiful," but overlook the last part, "But the laborers are few." In this verse, the *laborers* do not refer to pastors, evangelists, or missionaries, but to all of God's children. So, here's a reality check: Are all called to be pastors? No! Is everyone called to be an evangelist or a missionary? No, once more! Every one of us carries our kingdom assignment and purpose that we must carry out, so we are all these *laborers* who must gather the ripe harvest in our sphere of influence.

Again, the great commission mandate was given to all of God's children and was not limited to specific individuals with seminary degrees. The harvest is ripe in your neighborhood; it is ripe in your school; it is ripe in your workplace, and it is ripe all around you. What is missing is our recognition that we are the laborers who must enter our harvest field, which is our calling and sphere of influence.



## WHERE IS MY REWARD?

In the gospel of John, Jesus distinguishes between a shepherd and a hireling. The most significant difference is in the shepherd's heart attitude, in which the shepherd desires to serve others while the hireling desires to be served. The shepherd will say, "Here I am, Lord, send me," whereas the hireling will say, "Here I am, Lord, but send my neighbor." While the shepherd will gladly volunteer himself, the hireling will gladly volunteer someone else. And the shepherd is concerned with meeting the needs of others, whereas the hireling is concerned with meeting their own.

Our cultural society has done much harm, particularly through social media, which is grooming a generation that is basing their image and identity on the words, *me, myself,* and *I.* This mindset has also infiltrated every local church, where we have become more focused on ourselves, our personal needs, and how God can help us. The gospel mandate tells us to go into all the world, loving our neighbor and not neglecting the brokenhearted or the needy, which is a clear message that if you have been a child of God for a certain season, it is no longer about you, but about that one lost sheep that Jesus was telling us about.

Our kingdom reward will not be determined by how many Sunday services I have attended in my Christian life, how many Bible verses I have memorized, or how many different church programs I have participated in. Our kingdom reward will be determined by how you and I used our kingdom gift and time on this planet. And as we begin to serve others, we should not expect them to say "Thank you," to be praised by others, or even to be recognized in front of the church stage for our good works. Why? Because Jesus clearly stated, "But when you do a charitable deed, do not let your left hand know what your right hand is doing, that your charitable deed may be in secret; and your Father who sees in secret will Himself reward you openly."[2] And, in order to shift your focus away from yourself and toward others, you must first understand your true identity in Christ and your identity through Christ.

> **"Serve others from the bottom of your heart, not from the top of your credentials."**

# IDENTITY CRISIS

One of my favorite topics is discussing our kingdom's identity. The following statement has captivated and motivated me: Discover your identity *in* Christ and your identity *through* Christ. The concept of our God-given identity is so profound that the Lord moved my heart to the point where I published a book on the subject: *Can I See Your ID?*

The identity crisis epidemic is rife in our culture, as well as in the body of Christ as a whole. This identity crisis is frequently caused by the demonic belief that we are just average people who live an average life, have average opportunities, and achieve average results. This way of thinking is not only anti-biblical but also extremely destructive. And as long as you see yourself as an average person, you will feel insecure, uncertain, unstable, and have a victim mentality. When this happens, you will begin to believe that you are entitled to certain things and will begin to demand free handouts or that others need to serve you.

If you've been following the news on social media or through news networks, you've probably noticed a significant shift in our current culture, particularly among the younger generation, which is demanding free handouts from the government. And, sadly, the government has given in to their selfish demands. This similar heart attitude is not uncommon in our local churches, and it is largely due to the spiritual identity crisis that many Christians experience. In a nutshell, if you don't know your identity in Christ, you start acting, talking, and behaving like an immature Christian, expecting your local church and those within it to dance around your wants and needs. But if you know your identity in Christ, you automatically shift your focus away from yourself and your desires and toward others and their needs.

As I conclude this chapter, I fervently hope that you, my fellow brother, or sister in Christ, will discover your identity in Christ and then begin to discover your identity through Christ, which is your true purpose and calling on this earth. And as you discover who you are in Christ, the Holy Spirit will guide you in serving others and assisting others in either coming to Christ or understanding their identity in Christ. And as you begin to function in the area of servanthood, you will no longer be constrained by questions like, "Where is my reward?"

> *"Until you discover your identity in Christ and your identity through Christ, you will never be able to successfully influence or lead others."*

# CHAPTER 7
# THE SHEEP HAVE GONE ASTRAY

Recently, we have seen some prominent Christian figures abandon or even renounce their faith in God. When it comes to sheep going astray in the body of Christ, this is not a new phenomenon, but we are tragically witnessing a new trend among Christians, and this trend is almost becoming the norm.

When I was a young Christian, I easily mocked, discussed, and even used as illustrations in some of my sermons about those prominent Christians who fell into sin or were exposed by others. To be honest, talking about my fallen brothers and sisters in the Lord gave me a sense of spiritual satisfaction. But I'm thankful to my heavenly Father for His mercy and grace in not striking me down with sickness or other forms of punishment.

And the Holy Spirit had to teach me over the years how to function in love, grace, and intercession for such people who had fallen away. This was a powerful teachable moment for me, but the Lord has also begun to prompt my heart over the years to remind me that He is not only a God of love, mercy, and forgiveness, but He is also a righteous judge. Most of us cringe at the mere mention of the word *judge*, but if our heavenly Father did not exercise His righteous judgment, none of us would have any hope at all. And in this chapter, I hope you will see a healthy spiritual balance between God's love, righteousness, and discipline. Furthermore, how can you and I position our hearts to become true disciples of Jesus as He uses us to impact the lives of others, rather than becoming another victim of sin and eventually drifting away from God?

> *"Accepting Jesus into your heart is a once-in-a-lifetime act, but following Jesus is a daily lifestyle."*

## JESUS UNLEASHED

Most people have seen at least one painting or image of Jesus who had the appearance of a humble person with a gentle and appealing countenance. However, when I read the Bible, I come across a different kind of Jesus. When Jesus visited the temple and saw all the money changers and those who sold goods, it was one of the most classic moments of Jesus being unleashed. And in righteous rage, He flipped the tables, made a whip, and gave a heavenly butt whipping to the merchants. Now, this is the Jesus I know, and this is the Jesus that the church is currently misrepresenting in our culturally sensitive society.

I'm grateful for every local church, but what if Jesus appeared in front of your church on a Sunday morning? Would He clap, dance, and shout "Amen" in response to your pastor's sermon? Or will He take out His belt and begin whipping some spiritual butt-cheeks? That is a thought to ponder!

You see, when Jesus disrupted the business activities in the temple, His disciples did not complain or even question Him as to why He did what He did. The religious Pharisees, who represent our modern-day church leaders, were the only ones who objected to this unorthodox behavior. With that said, I'm not trying to disparage our fellow pastors or church leaders; rather, I'd like to point out that throughout Jesus' brief ministry, He primarily clashed with the religious leaders of His day.

Pastors and church leaders nowadays have a lot on their plates, and with vast changes in politics, society, and culture, it sometimes appears impossible for them to properly release the Word of God so that it does not offend others while speaking the truth in love. But, at the end of the day, the church leadership must remain vigilant and full of Holy Spirit discernment, because the antichrist and the Jezebel virus are infiltrating the doors of the body of Christ like never before. And the sole reason Jesus began cleaning out the temple is the same reason He is preparing His whip to clean out the worldly junk that has infiltrated Christ's body. Yes, Jesus is constantly pouring out His love, mercy, and grace, but He is also pouring out His righteous judgment.

> *"The discipline of our heavenly Father is like a daily multi-vitamin for our spirit man."*

# WHY SO MANY LAMB CHOPS?

There's something savory about biting into a juicy lamb chop. Sorry, Christian vegans, but if you stick around for a few more paragraphs, you'll be able to grasp the spiritual implication without chewing me out. It's fascinating that Jesus is frequently referred to as the Lamb of God, and that we are referred to as His sheep. He was the Lamb who was sacrificed eternally for our salvation and redemption. And we were all scattered and lost sheep in the absence of a shepherd.

The question of why we have so many lamb chops is not about Christ, but about the body of Christ and why so many believers have become lamb chops on Satan's plate, who is constantly looking for whom he can devour. The enemy of our soul has been viciously attacking and hunting down God's children like never before because he knows his time is limited, and he is pouring out his demonic confusion with such potency that what is right has become wrong, and what was wrong has now been accepted as right.

Why, once again, are there so many lamb chops on Satan's plate? One of the main reasons why many Christians end up on the devil's plate is that they choose the broad path of life and are unwilling to become true disciples of Jesus Christ. The Bible differentiates between the broad and narrow paths, and it also clearly states the cost of being a disciple of Jesus. And, sadly, instead of following the Lamb of God, many end up as lamb chops in Satan's mouth.

The important thing to remember here is that every born-again believer must make a firm decision to believe in the fullness of God's Word and fully commit themselves to serve the Lord. And if we follow the Lamb of God who is also the Lion of Judah wholeheartedly, we will not end up as victims on the devil's plate. And if the devil tries to attack you, we can always rely on the Lion of Judah.

> *"True shepherds understand that they must sacrifice their personal time and desires to serve others, whereas hirelings look for any excuse to focus on themselves."*

## ARE YOU A SHEPHERD OR A HIRELING?

In the previous chapter, I have already discussed the difference between the shepherd and a hireling, where the great distinction has to do with the attitude of the heart. But, in this case, I'd like to go a step further and highlight the role and responsibilities of a true shepherd.

True shepherds must be motivated by the fear of the Lord rather than the fear of man. Furthermore, true shepherds believe that "the higher the climb, the greater the victory," whereas hirelings believe that "the higher the climb, the greater the fall." This emphasizes the distinction between a genuine kingdom shepherd and someone who carries a title.

Shepherds cannot or should not be limited to pastors alone; this divine principle applies to any born-again believer who desires to live a life of purpose as they carry out their kingdom assignment. To honestly answer the question, "Am I a shepherd or a hireling?" you must examine your heart, spirit man, and motives before the Lord and allow the Holy Spirit to reveal to you and me what is going on internally. And as He does so, we must either repent before Him or thank Him for His grace and mercy in our lives as He faithfully continues to entrust us with His kingdom mandate on this earth.

> **"The true shepherd (disciple) is always looking for ways to serve others, whereas the hireling (religious person) is always looking for ways to be served."**

## JESUS WAS A LIFE COACH AND A MENTOR

Jesus did not construct any structures, programs, or ministries; instead, He focused on developing the inner leadership character of His disciples through personal life coaching and mentorship. The healings, miracles, and supernatural things that Jesus did were incredible, but they were limited to those specific individuals because not everyone needed healing or was present during some of Jesus' supernatural deeds. However, Jesus' discipleship of His inner circle disciples and those who followed Him has continued to spiritually ricochet from generation to generation to this day.

Remember that not everyone will be supernaturally healed or even require healing, but everyone who is born-again must become a disciple of Christ and be mentored and equipped by others in order to become well-equipped and trained followers of Jesus Christ. And understanding Jesus as a life coach and personal mentor to His twelve disciples is critical for us to understand as God's children and church leaders.

This is one of the reasons I'm so passionate about discipleship through coaching and mentorship because you can touch and impact the individual on a personal level, and it's why whenever someone gives their life to the Lord, we direct them towards discipleship and water baptism, which is a critical next step in their spiritual growth in the Lord.

One of the reasons small groups or home groups are so successful is that they are similar to what Jesus did with His disciples. Frequently, Jesus would be in remote areas with His twelve disciples around a campfire, or on numerous boat trips, or visiting many homes, and in all of these endeavors, the twelve disciples traveled with Him and gained firsthand experience from Jesus, who became their life coach and mentor.

If your local church does not have a discipleship program, school, or classes, you should not be surprised if there is a high turnover rate or if many people struggle in their personal walk with the Lord. And if you truly want to see others grow spiritually and walk in their kingdom assignment, make discipleship a top priority. And if the shepherds in their local churches follow in Christ's footsteps, fewer sheep will go astray.

> **"Choose today to become a Godly and a kingdom role model to the next generation."**

# CHAPTER 8
# UN-BRAINWASHING THE BRAINWASHED

I've heard the sarcastic gesture, "You're being brainwashed," on several occasions and in various contexts throughout my life. And in one specific situation, I once replied with a big smile, "Yes, you are correct, my brain is being washed from all of the brainwashings that I have received over these years."

So, what does it mean to un-brainwash those who have been brainwashed? This question refers to hard-core theological doctrines as well as what is going on in our current society. I once heard a sermon in which the preacher said, "The reason I am a Baptist is because Baptists are the most theologically and biblically sound in comparison to other denominations." My main concern was not with the preacher's statement, no matter how true or false it was, but with the word "Baptist."

The preacher's remarks are nothing new or surprising, but they do highlight my subsequent point that we as God's children place so much emphasis on our theology, our manmade traditions, or our denominational beliefs that we stray away from the original Source, who is Christ. And, because of our ignorance, we are unaware of how doctrines or theological concepts that do not edify or add value to others have brainwashed us. Consider this: when people look at you, do they see a Baptist, a Catholic, a Charismatic, a Methodist, a Pentecostal, or a child of God?

I was raised in a very strict and conservative Pentecostal background, and I frequently look back and evaluate many aspects of theology, sermons, "do's" and "do nots," and other rigid manmade traditions to only thank the Lord for His grace, revelations, and mercy over my life, and that my children did not have to grow up in a similar religious environment. Yes, there was plenty of religious brainwashing during my teenage years, but when I married, my wife and I decided to get un-brainwashed from all the manmade ideologies, theologies, and doctrines that had been bombarding us all those years.

As much as this was our personal decision to embark on a journey of discovering our God-given identity and purpose, I continue to meet believers from all over who are still bound by religious ideologies and strongholds. Some of these people I've known for a long time, and it breaks my heart to see them exist as a child of God but not live as a child of God.

"If only I had access to social media and all of the available resources that we have today to help you grow more in the Lord and to help you in the ministry, then I would not have gone through so many challenges and struggles in my spiritual growth and while I was in the youth ministry," I often find myself saying to someone from the younger generation. Having said that, my heavenly Father saw my heart, as well as the hearts of many others in a similar situation, and still released His rhema Word into our hearts and spirit man.

And the primary goal of this chapter is to assist you in fully re-evaluating your spiritual thinking, theological beliefs, and in becoming un-brainwashed from all of the brainwashing that you may have received throughout your years as a child of God. This way, with renewed hearts and minds, we can all effectively serve one another and work together to build God's kingdom on earth.

> *"Renewing our heart and mind is a daily discipline, not a one-time occurrence."*

## WHAT ARE YOU DOING WITH THE KINGDOM KEYS THAT WERE ENTRUSTED TO YOU?

Years ago, there was a verse in the Bible that changed my thinking and allowed me to position myself in the proper spiritual adjustment so that I could become an asset and a valuable tool in the hands of my heavenly Father. This profound passage was spoken by Jesus as He rebuked the religious leaders, saying, "What sorrow awaits you experts in religious law! For you remove the key to knowledge from the people. You don't enter the Kingdom, and you prevent others from entering."[1] This is still happening tragically in the body of Christ, where God's children are bound by fear, legalism, man-made doctrines, and a plethora of denominational creeds.

Those with eyes to see, ears to hear, and an open heart to understand that our current culture is brainwashing the younger generation through social media, academia, and new laws and regulations that are spewing from politics. Today, the younger generation is more concerned with climate change and global warming than with fighting for the rights of the unborn, and academia has shifted dramatically from grooming a future generation of influential, successful, responsible, and accountable individuals to grooming them into sensitive crybabies who are in full tantrum mode and demanding free stuff. By the minute, these priceless souls are being brainwashed.

With that said, there is a larger issue in the body of Christ where believers are more concerned with revival than having their theological thinking reformed. We have people praying and fasting for the next great outpouring on our land, which I believe will happen, but what they or the church need is a great washing of their spiritually blinded eyes. Many believers are also stuck on denominational structures, theological creeds, and traditional beliefs. And while they are praying, going to church, and fighting for their doctrinal beliefs, the world is going to hell in a handbasket; academia is brainwashing our children; politicians are passing legislation and new immoral laws, and the media is preaching a more appealing gospel message than the local church. Why? Because the body of Christ and the local church have strayed from its original spiritual mandate. This is not meant to be a rebuke, but rather a warning, because we complain about all the brainwashing that occurs in culture, media, schools, and society, but we tend to overlook how much spiritual brainwashing occurs in many churches and many denominations.

Every child of God and every local church has kingdom keys that have been entrusted to us all by our heavenly Father, but what we do with them is entirely up to us. This reminds me of a funny anecdote that goes like this:

*A thief breaks into a house and hears, "Jesus is watching you!" as he walks through the living room. He looks around and sees no one. He then enters the master bedroom and hears again, "Jesus is watching you!" The thief becomes concerned and begins to follow where he allegedly heard that voice, and as he enters the kitchen, he sees a parrot and hears the same phrase, "Jesus is watching you!" But this time he realized it was the parrot who was speaking to him. "I'm not a Christian, and I don't believe in Jesus!" says the thief, relieved. And the parrot quickly responded, "Jesus is the name of our Rottweiler."*

This amusing anecdote speaks volumes about what I'm trying to convey in this crucial chapter, which is that we should not be unaware that our children, youth, and the younger generation are watching us, even if we don't know or notice it. They are paying close attention to our theology, church services, programs, church politics, theological debates, and sermons delivered from our pulpits. And if we are not careful, we will be grooming a generation of Baptists, Charismatics, Pentecostals, and Methodists who will be full of denominational theology rather than the Holy Spirit and the living Word of God. And we do have the kingdom keys, and now is the time to start unlocking the kingdom potential that is sitting dormant in the hearts of the younger generation.



## UN-BRAINWASHING THE BRAINWASHED

For my wife and me, being a father of three has been a Six Flags experience. And, especially with my seventeen-year-old son, it can feel like you're on an endless rollercoaster ride. He would approach me from time to time with various thoughts, remarks, statements, or curiosity questions. After carefully listening to some of his strange or teenage nonsense, I would frequently ask, "Where did you hear that?" Alternatively, "Who told you that?" And it was usually someone's remarks from a classmate, a friend, or what he saw on social media.

It may appear normal for any teenager to be on a path of personal discovery and trying to understand life, but as parents, we know all too well that as our teenage son or daughter matures, they will encounter plenty of foolish nonsense. With that said, much brainwashing occurs during the process, and we as parents have been commanded by God to assist in guiding our son or daughter down the path of truth and imparting some wisdom that comes from the living Word of God. In other words, we need to help them un-brainwash themselves from all of the brainwashings they are subjected to on a daily basis.

As much as this may appear to be a normal family process or procedure, parents do tend to neglect this critical area and simply brush off the teenage nonsense that is coming from their child's lips. When a parent ignores such critical moments, they allow worldly nonsense to captivate and eventually consume the child's heart and mind, which often turns into a belief or even an ideology. Then we marvel at how the younger generation appears to be brainwashed, and why so many local churches struggle to connect with or impact the younger generation.

You've probably noticed a pattern throughout this book and all of my previous books where I always make time to talk about our children and the younger generation because they are the church of tomorrow, and they will be the ones that the Lord will use very powerfully to usher in the next great awakening and revival that many are preaching and praying about. And it is for this reason that we, as parents and kingdom leaders, must take the living Word of God and, with the help of the Holy Spirit and His anointing, un-brainwash the hearts and minds of the younger generations, so they will understand that they have a kingdom purpose on this earth. And this is one of the most important aspects of discipleship, where we apply the Word of God with the Holy Spirit to the hearts and minds of God's children, washing away all worldly and demonic pollution in the process.

> *"Your mind is similar to a womb. What you sow into it determines what you will produce in your life."*

# CHAPTER 9

# PLEASE FOLLOW THE ORIGINAL SCRIPT

Movies have a specific outlined script, and each actor or actress in a movie must adhere to a specific script. Manuals also contain detailed instructions that must be followed. Builders must abide by every detail specified on the building plans. And the same is true when it comes to us complying, submitting, and following every word written in the manual known as the Bible.

Have you ever built kitchen cabinets, furniture, or other items that came with a detailed instruction manual? Have you ever inadvertently skipped a step or forgotten a detail, only to discover that what you were building did not turn out as planned? Let's face it, we've all been there! One of the most inconvenient aspects of this occurrence is that we usually have to undo what we built and go back to where we skipped that specific step.

You see, when the original manufacturer created a specific product, they also included a detailed manual with detailed instructions that we must strictly follow. If we choose to disregard the recommended instructions, we are fully responsible if the product does not look right or does not function as intended. Worse, we can sometimes damage the product because we choose not to follow the instructions.

This is also true in the case of discipleship. The Word of God is the original manual written by our Creator, and this manual is detailed in all aspects of salvation, healing, righteousness, spiritual growth, calling, forgiveness, and making disciples. Having said that, we have decided to deviate from the original script! Why? Because we believe we are fully capable of taking matters into our own hands because we have been Christians for so long.

First of all, when we try to find scriptural references in the Bible that relate to discipleship, we do have to begin with Jesus. And the most powerful commandment, which we call the *Great Commission* that we have received from the mouth of the Lord as He said, "Go therefore and make disciples of all the nations."[1] And we should keep in mind that Jesus chose twelve core disciples for Himself, and many more disciples followed Him throughout His brief ministry on earth.

The Bible is not afraid to mention numerous occasions, situations, teachable moments, hands-on experiences, and practical life lessons in relation to discipleship and discipleship making. And the four gospels offer a broad perspective and outline to numerous stories and situations that offer us powerful applications that we can apply in our personal lives as well as our kingdom assignment on this earth.

When my wife and I moved to the peachy state of Georgia in 2013, we both knew that Free Chapel would be our new spiritual home. And, during our first year there, we learned about their School of Discipleship (SOD), about which our friends boasted. We signed up without hesitation, and less than two years later, we both graduated.

During our discipleship schooling, we would frequently have great conversations as we drove back home, reflecting on what we had learned that day. "Honey, I grew up in church most of my life, but I was never taught these basic fundamentals as they relate to my faith in Christ," I'd say. "Can you imagine how much legalism we've accumulated in such a short time!" Or, "Wow, I wish I had known these things when I was a youth pastor!"

One thing that struck us both was how practical and simple discipleship was, and how, despite the fact that we had both been in ministry and as believers for many years, this discipleship school revolutionized our theological thinking and brought us to a whole new spiritual level. And I'm grateful to God and to the pastoral leadership of SOD for transforming my perspective and understanding of discipleship. This is not only my personal testimony but also the testimony of thousands of others who have attended this same discipleship school.

I do want to emphasize a much more important point here. It's not a cute Christian term or a catchy phrase that we use in our churches when it comes to discipleship. Discipleship is a way of life for us! Why? Because we are followers of our Lord Jesus Christ. Remember, if Jesus is our Rock, discipleship is the Rock on which we build, just as you would do house framing on top of a concrete foundation.

Could you imagine pouring only the foundation and then living on it without any walls, roof, windows, or other structural features that come with a new house? As strange as it may sound, many Christians accept Christ as their Lord and Savior and then stop there. Again, it's the same as living solely on a concrete foundation with no walls or roof and becoming vulnerable and exposed to life's various storms.

Too many believers have become casualties and continue to be subjected to demonic attacks and various life temptations, becoming victims rather than victors. As a result, being a disciple of Christ is critical, and discipleship is not a one-time event in which you receive a certificate of completion and are set for life. Certainly not! We are Christ's disciples, and we must continue to be His disciples by constantly growing. Remember that a disciple is a student, and as spiritual students, our official graduation will take place the day we die on this earth. And as you venture through this chapter, you will understand why we must stick to the originality of the living scriptures rather than succumbing to watered-down sermons.

> *"Jesus did not bring a religion to the earth, but rather His kingdom. So, what are you constructing in your spiritual life, ministry, and the local church?"*

# CAN YOU PLEASE ITCH MY EARS AND TICKLE MY TOES?

"For a time is coming when people will no longer listen to sound and wholesome teaching. They will follow their own desires and will look for teachers who will tell them whatever their itching ears want to hear. They will reject the truth and chase after myths."[2] These two verses are very sobering, but they are even more so today than they were in Apostle Paul's day.

When I study the Bible or write books, I frequently refer to different versions of the Bible to gain a deeper or broader perspective of what I'm reading or what message I'm trying to convey to the reader. My favorite Bible version is the New King James Version (NKJV), but I also like to use the AMP, NIV, NLT, and MSG. And what's even more amazing is that there are over sixty different biblical translations available for us to use as references or for personal study. That is incredible! In recent years, however, I've noticed new and contemporary Bible versions being read by fellow Christians in local churches. They are as follows:

- **NSSV** – *New Seeker Sensitive Version* (The gospel of Comfort)
- **TMYV** – *Tickle My Ears Version* (The gospel of Half-Truths)
- **NQJV** – *New Queen Jamie Version* (The gospel of Feminism)
- **MMV** – *My Message Version* (The gospel of Opinions)

- **LGBT** – *Love Grace Blessing Translation* (The gospel of Inclusiveness)
- **SAB** – *Super Amplified Bible* (The gospel of Everything)
- **MPDB** – *My Preferred Denomination Bible* (The gospel of Manmade Traditions)
- **SMV** – *Social Media Version* (The gospel of Confusion)
- **FWV** – *Free Will Version* (The gospel of Do Whatever You Feel Is Right)
- **DHMF** – *Don't Hurt My Feelings* (The gospel of Feelings)
- **#MEV** – *#MeVersion* (The gospel of It's All About Me)

You might be laughing right now, or you might be scratching your head in puzzlement. In any case, those who consider the original text to be outdated, legalistic, or irrelevant are pushing for the above new Bible versions. In what way? Many people believe that the original Word is too masculine because it frequently uses the word *man* to refer to both genders. Alternatively, there are many evangelical Christians, particularly among the younger generation, who sincerely believe that God created gays or who fully support the LGBTQ lifestyle. Why? Because they genuinely believe that God created them in this manner!

This is not a new phenomenon, as Christians or believers have fallen victim to various heresies or doctrinal errors throughout history, but this time this type of belief or ideology has reached new heights. In one of the chapters of my book, *Can I See Your ID?*, I discuss *The Truth vs Your Opinions.* In this section, I discuss how we as Christians tend to lean more toward our own opinions rather than the truth of God's Word. And the tragic issue here is that the more we rely on our own opinions, those opinions eventually become our truth, and the truth of God's Word simply becomes an opinion.

This is dangerous, and it has also perplexed many Christian believers who have allowed their personal opinions to take precedence over the truth of God's Word. And if we are not careful, we will allow the reckless and immoral culture to redefine God's Word and restructure the way we have church, and raise transformational disciples for God's kingdom. And as God's children, we must train our spiritual ears to hear what the Holy Spirit is saying to us all in this season of life.

> *"The true essence of discipleship is introducing others to the King and His kingdom, rather than your denomination or religious traditions."*

## SIGNS AND SYMPTOMS OF UNHEALTHY DISCIPLESHIP

When you experience pain or discomfort in your body, it is a sign that something is wrong! When you see one of those bright yellow or red lights on your car's dashboard, you know it's trying to tell you something. Similarly, the Holy Spirit who dwells within us prompts us with specific warnings, discernment, or inner checks to what He wants us to pay attention to.

There is no such thing as a perfect church or ministry! There are no pastors or ministers who are endowed with infinite wisdom, knowledge, or comprehension! And no single church has the best and most accurate discipleship program or curriculum! However, if you are sensitive to the Holy Spirit and have a genuine hunger for God's Word, you will be able to recognize the signs and symptoms of unhealthy discipleship.

It's no secret that not every church has a discipleship training program, or that their current discipleship is out of date and irrelevant. Those who do have solid programs or curriculums may not be teaching the entire truth in order to avoid scaring new converts or causing church fallout. Let's take a closer look at some of the most visible signs and symptoms of unhealthy discipleship, for example:

- Not teaching or emphasizing that hell exists and that many people go there.
- Choosing the least offensive bits and pieces from the Bible.
- It bears repeating that if the Bible mentions something as sin or sinful, it is a sin.
- Avoiding topics that are sensitive, controversial, politically incorrect, or offensive.
- Ignoring the immorality and demonic activities that are occurring in our culture and society.

- Focusing solely on God's grace, mercy, favor, blessing, and prosperity.

The above is only a brief summary of a much longer list of situations in which we would rather avoid hurting someone's feelings than challenge them to live a holy life. But if we stick to the original script, we automatically position our life, family, local church, or ministry into a healthy kingdom alignment and will reap tremendous rewards.

So, my friend, I sincerely challenge you to stick to the original script, which is the living Word of God, regardless of the cost or how uncomfortable you may make others feel around you. Our current culture and various political laws are attempting to erase the fundamental biblical principles that were established in our country hundreds of years ago. We can make a kingdom difference on this earth if we stick to the original script.

> *"If you talk, look, dress, and act like an Adventist, a Baptist, a Catholic, a Charismatic, a Methodist, or a Pentecostal, you will make disciples in your image, not in the image of Christ."*

# CHAPTER 10
# POLITICIANS, THEOLOGIANS, OR KINGDOM AMBASSADORS?

I have been known for being politically incorrect, especially on social media, where I ruffled a lot of political feathers. But this time, I want to direct my attention to my fellow brothers and sisters in Christ, hoping to ruffle some angelic feathers by capturing the attention of your hearts and spirit man rather than the political ideology that has spread like a cancerous blanket in the body of Christ.

I won't get political with you in this chapter because that isn't the point of the book, which is titled *Politicians, Theologians, or Kingdom Ambassadors?* What exactly does this mean? I'm glad you inquired! Something unprecedented occurred within the body of Christ during our most recent presidential elections in 2016 and 2020. Millions of Christians became politicians rather than kingdom ambassadors. This remark was not meant to be amusing, but rather to be very concerning.

We are responsible and accountable as citizens of a country for being aware of our political sphere and participating in the voting process. Having said that, many Christians choose not to vote but do engage in political discourse. However, during and especially after President

Trump's election, there was a dramatic shift in the body of Christ and among many Christians. Everyone became politically engaged and active suddenly. On the one hand, this is a good thing, but the current results have been disastrous.

The body of Christ has never been more divided or stirred up as it has been before, and this time it is due to politics. To be honest, it doesn't matter whether you lean right or left, or whether you wear a blue shirt or a red shirt; everyone has the right to their political beliefs, but I want to shift our attention away from politics and back to kingdom thinking. Before we engage or become involved in the political sphere, we must first recognize that we are kingdom ambassadors, and only then can we choose whether to wear red or blue glasses. But, sadly, this has not been the case.

Millions of Christians in America have chosen to forego their ambassadorship and lay aside their daily cross in favor of donning their favorite political color, grabbing a political sign, and shouting in the faces of their fellow believers. Many people have put their bibles aside and pulled out their political manuals. And, instead of becoming kingdom-active in their communities or local churches, many have become more politically active in various groups or organizations. Uh oh, I'm seeing a lot of angelic feathers flying around right now!

As we progress through this chapter, I challenge you to honestly examine your heart to determine whether you and I are representing ourselves as politicians, theologians, or kingdom ambassadors on this earth.

## ARE WE GIVING OUT KINGDOM PASSPORTS OR SEMINARY CERTIFICATES?

As it hangs on the wall, a certificate looks nice inside a fancy frame. However, this certificate will not allow you to enter foreign countries or territories. Any ambassador who does not have a valid passport will be denied entry into any country. And now I'd like to pose a unique question to you: Are we issuing kingdom passports or seminary certificates?

I recently attended a large youth conference in South Carolina where I had the opportunity to interact with people I had never met before. During one of these group discussions, one pastor expressed his disappointment with Franklin Graham, saying, "I'm a little disappointed with Franklin Graham, because he is not following in the footsteps of his father Billy, and he has entangled himself in politics instead of preaching the gospel." Those who don't know me well enough are unaware that certain words, phrases, or statements will set off my spiritual antenna. Without any hesitation, I responded, "What makes you think that Franklin Graham is not preaching the gospel through the political sphere that he is currently engaged in?" My response elicited a brief pause among this group of people.

I then began to elaborate on what I meant and related to the entire group that God wants to use us beyond the walls of the church, especially in this politically divided nation, and that we can use more credible and influential voices in the political sphere, to which the group agreed. And with that said, I'm grateful that someone like Franklin Graham is taking a bold stance in the political arena by defending our religious rights and portraying himself as an ambassador of God's kingdom rather than a politician.

To take it a step further, I find it appalling and surprising that so many pastors and prominent Christian leaders are remaining silent on the issue of politics, policies, and the political turmoil brewing in our country. And I'm not referring to the political turmoil in the body of Christ, which is severe, but to the level of hostility directed at our Christian faith and biblical views. We have a large number of government officials who are attempting to silence us and shut us down by enacting legislation that restricts, controls, or makes it illegal for us to freely practice or live out our faith in this country.

Furthermore, these same pastors or church leaders are being too politically correct by not speaking out against these laws, legislations, or demonic propaganda that is attempting to bulldoze its way through the body of Christ. And Jesus has a word for those who seek to please others rather than serve as kingdom ambassadors, "Also I say to you, whoever confesses Me before men, him the Son of Man also will confess before the angels of God. But he who denies Me before men will be denied before the angels of God."[1]

The time has come for Christians who choose to be politically correct to find themselves on the wrong side of history, as the Bible warns us, "And He will set the sheep on His right hand, but the goats on his left."[2] You get to choose which side you want to be on. Either to the right or the left. And being a kingdom ambassador on this earth entails operating under the kingdom passport, which is the Word of God, rather than our man-made and religious seminary certificates. And we must also provide every believer with these kingdom passports, which will enable them to serve as needed kingdom ambassadors on this planet.

> *"A disciple of Christ has King David's mindset and heart, which is shepherding others, whereas a religious person has King Saul's mindset and heart, which is power and authority over others."*

## I CHOOSE TO BE A KINGDOM AMBASSADOR

In his second epistle to the church of Corinth, Apostle Paul used a unique word that we often overlook when he said, "Now then, we are ambassadors for Christ, as though God were pleading through us."[3] It is also important to note that Paul used the word *we* to refer to all of us.

When you and I grasp the revelation of what it means to be a kingdom ambassador, we will begin to position our heart, mind, and purpose on this earth as Christ's ambassadors, rather than religious individuals. This is also a decision that we must all make. Being a typical Christian churchgoer is a choice, as is becoming an influential kingdom ambassador on this earth. Furthermore, being a kingdom ambassador will drastically distinguish you from others in that your speech will be different, your thinking will not be of this secular world, your behavior and lifestyle will also distinguish you from others, and your actions and deeds will be supernaturally backed up by the kingdom of heaven, leaving others speechless. And, my prayer, my friend, is that we all choose to be kingdom ambassadors, laying aside our political ideologies and theological certificates to represent the kingdom of God on this earth.

> *"If you don't stand for something, then you will eventually fall for anything."*

# CHAPTER 11
# 95/5 PRINCIPLE

What is the 95/5 Principle? This will be one of my Stanology principles, which will be defined or interpreted differently by others. The 95/5 Principle is the fundamental distinction that categorizes born-again Christians as either 95 percent or 5 percent. The 95 percent refers to those who are called or carry out a kingdom assignment outside of their local church's ministry walls. These people have a mission and a calling in the marketplace, entrepreneurship, academia, media, arts & entertainment, politics, or the news media. However, the remaining 5 percent work full-time in their local church or on mission fields as missionaries and evangelists. Or those who have a full-time ministry platform where they primarily focus on preaching, teaching, or evangelizing the gospel message through social media, video, podcasts, conferences, and seminars, and traveling around the world, and are fully funded through financial donations.

This principle may be nothing new or even surprising to some, but there is a reason why I decided to devote an entire chapter to it. Over the years, I've encountered many preachers, sermons, teachings, and fellow Christians who have a limited, even legalistic understanding of the church's role and the function of every believer on this earth. And in this unique chapter, let us delve a little deeper into the 95/5 Principle.



## ARE WE RAISING MINISTERS OR KINGDOM AMBASSADORS?

The question of whether you or your local church is raising ministers or kingdom ambassadors may be contentious and theologically unsound for some religious folks to grasp. Yes, we are all ministers of the gospel, but I wanted to highlight a misconception that many Christians may have.

"We need to raise and disciple more pastors, missionaries, church leaders, evangelists, street ministers, and those whom the Lord would send all over the world to preach the gospel message," I've heard many times from the pulpit, at conferences, and seminars, in books and blogs, on social media, and YouTube. There is some truth to the above statements that pastors, preachers, or Christians like to make in general, but all of the above is primarily limited to the 5 percent category. What about the remaining 95 percent?

There is a big difference between raising or discipling someone to be a religious minister or training them to be a kingdom ambassador. A *minister* is someone who performs religious services in front of an individual or a congregation. An *ambassador*, on the other hand, is a high-ranking diplomatic official who represents the interests of a government, a country, or a nation. There is a significant difference between a minister's functionality, responsibilities, and influence and that of an ambassador.

Apostle Paul provides for us additional insight into the importance of knowing the difference between a minister and an ambassador when he said, "I am in chains now, still preaching this message as God's ambassador."[1] Paul's statement was not identifying himself as a pastor, or an evangelist, or even a missionary, but as an ambassador who represents a King and a kingdom.

This divine principle is not difficult to understand. All we have to do is teach and disciple others as kingdom ambassadors, and if those individuals feel called to full-time ministry within a local church or in the mission fields, they can transition further into that sphere in the process. And, once again, in his letter to the church of Corinth, Apostle Paul provided additional clarity, "There are diversities of gifts, but the same Spirit. There are differences of ministries, but the same Lord. And there are diversities of activities, but it is the same God who works all in all."[2]

He continues to elaborate on this same thought, "And God has appointed these in the church: first apostles, second prophets, third teachers, after that miracles, then gifts of healings, helps, administrations, varieties of tongues. *Are* all apostles? *Are* all prophets? *Are* all teachers? *Are* all workers of miracles? Do all have gifts of healings? Do all speak with tongues? Do all interpret? But earnestly desire the best gifts. And yet I show you a more excellent way."[3]

The concept here is that each of us has different gifts and different kingdom assignments, and it is critical that we understand this truth as well as be able to teach and disciple others so that they can discover and understand their gifts and calling. Our main focus as the body of Christ and as each local church should always be to raise kingdom ambassadors, and the process the Holy Spirit will direct each and every child of God towards their kingdom purpose and assignment.

> *"True biblical discipleship is not about cloning others into your own image, but to help others to discover their own identity and purpose."*

## AGENT OR A VICTIM OF CHANGE?

Change is a phenomenon that has occurred and will continue to occur throughout history and as time passes. Change is essential! Change is required! And change serves a divine purpose of its own. On the other hand, change can have destructive connotations, especially if it is driven by a demonic agenda, with the goal of opposing God's perfect will on earth or smearing the credibility and authenticity of God's Holy Word.

The Word of God never changes, yet it is constantly creating new things, or at least we as His children are constantly in awe of all the new things that we encounter during our brief life on this planet. And whether I am an agent of change or a victim of change will be determined solely by whether I am fulfilling my kingdom purpose and calling. For example, if a child of God is confused or has not yet discovered their assignment and purpose for what God has called them to, then when God begins to change the spiritual seasons or significantly shift the body of Christ in another direction, many so-called Christians become victims of this change, rather than agents (ambassadors) who have positioned themselves to execute this change on this earth.

My fellow brothers and sisters in Christ, I fervently desire for all of you to discover and understand your divine purpose on earth and what your heavenly Father has called you to do, so that we will not be pew warmers thinking that the Lord has only equipped the 5 percent to fulfill His will on earth, be those who are also the other 95 percent who have a great kingdom assignment. And together, as the 100 percent body of Christ, we will be able to do and accomplish much more.

> **"You will either become an agent of change or become a victim to change."**

# CHAPTER 12

# THE CAT HAS GROWN INTO A LION

You wake up one ordinary morning, make yourself a cup of coffee, and walk out onto your deck to admire the splendor of a beautiful sunrise. And as you sip your coffee, you notice your neighbor is playing with cute-looking furry animals in his yard. As you approach your neighbor, you smile and say, "Good morning, neighbor, it's another beautiful morning, isn't it?" "It sure is!" he responds. "Are those new kittens you just got?" you inquire. "Nope, they're baby lions!" he says. And then, perplexed, you ask, "Why in the world did you get yourself lion cubs?" "I'm going to raise them and train them to kill, and when they're ready, I'm going to release them into your yard, so they can kill and devour your children!" your neighbor responds without a heartbeat.

Some of you may be baffled as to whether you are reading a Stephen King thriller novel or a book on discipleship! Yes, this is a discipleship book, and I just wanted to draw attention to one of the most thought-provoking passages in the Bible, where Apostle Peter stated, "Stay alert! Watch out for your great enemy, the devil. He prowls around like a roaring lion, looking for someone to devour."[1]

The preceding introductory illustration serves as a sober reminder that the enemy of our soul, the devil, is

83

constantly on the lookout for his next victim, and those precious victims are frequently our children and the younger generation. With that said, one of the problems here is that we are aware that the devil is a vicious lion, but we are blinded by the fact that all we see are cute little furry baby lions that appear so friendly and harmless, without realizing that these cute furballs will eventually grow into treacherous lions thirsty for innocent blood. And in this chapter, I want to awaken our spiritual discernment so that we, as parents or church leaders, are not blind to the fact that this roaring lion is viciously attacking our children and the younger generation.

> **"Know the difference between the Lion of Judah and the devouring lion."**

## MOMMY AND DADDY, CAN I KEEP THIS CUTE KITTEN?

Being a father of three has been a tremendous blessing, and it's always a wonderful feeling when your child asks you for something they believe will bring them pleasure, satisfaction, or fulfillment. But, as parents, we are also aware that not everything is beneficial to your child, regardless of age or gender. The privileges and challenges of parenting include always trying to strike a healthy balance between what you say yes to and when you have to say no. Whether your son or daughter agrees with your response or not, as a parent, you must make the final decision.

For example, if your child requests that you buy a pet cat or dog for them, you may do so. But if they ask you to buy a python snake, you're probably going to say no! If your son asks you to buy him a basketball, you will gladly oblige for the sake of getting them outside and away from video games. However, if your son asks you to buy him a handgun, you will be extremely hesitant.

The serpent of old is unleashing all of his cunning tactics and strategies against God's children like never before. And one of these strategies is offering us a small-sized baby lion in the form of cultural shift; societal acceptance; diversity; inclusiveness; gender identity; sexual revolution; and at first, those things may appear harmless until they bear fruit, and before we realize this baby lion has now transformed into a devouring monster.

Here's an eye-opening example to prove my point: It began innocently enough as Civil Union, then evolved into gay marriage, then legal rights for homosexuals, and now it is the law of the land. Another example: It started with gender identity, then it progressed to changing the bathroom signs, and now there are laws and regulations in place to support boys or pedophiles entering a girls' bathroom. Another example: It began as a way to discover who you are, then evolved into scientific and educational doctrine, and now an eight-year-old can have a sex change. All of the preceding is only a sketch of this innocent lion cub, which will eventually grow into a vicious lion as it devours the innocent hearts and minds of our children and the younger generation.

As spiritual shepherds and parents, we are called to be the watchman, standing guard on the walls of our families and local churches, keeping our spiritual eyes and ears open. The enemy of our soul is constantly looking for new ways to deceive mankind, especially God's children, but thank God for the Holy Spirit who dwells within us and can expose these disguised cute kittens for what they truly are. And, yes, mom and dad, there will be times when you must tell your son or daughter, "No, you cannot keep this cute kitten!"

> **"Deception will appear appealing on the outside, like a sweet candy, but it will be filled with deadly poison on the inside."**

## CONFORMED OR TRANSFORMED?

People in the body of Christ are increasingly being conformed to the ideology and doctrine of the worldly culture, rather than being transformed by the Word of God and the power of the Holy Spirit. And the Book of Romans makes a bold declaration, stating, "And do not be conformed to this world, but be transformed by the renewing of your mind, that you may prove what *is* that good and acceptable and perfect will of God."[2]

For example, when it comes to pro-life or pro-choice issues, a surprising number of Christians are either neutral or lean toward the belief that it is everyone's personal choice to do whatever they want. When it comes to the sanctity of marriage, many people are afraid to speak out in support of traditional views for fear of being labeled as a righteous zealot. And many Christians have been silenced in recent years by the hot social issues of LGBTQ, gender pronouns, transgenderism, drag queens, and bathroom laws. All of the above are contentious issues, and sadly, many Christians are keeping their mouths shut, not for fear of being mocked or persecuted, but for a lack of inner convictions.

I've been very active on the social media platform for a while and have networked with a few thousand pastors, ministers, and church leaders, and to my surprise, there is only a small handful of them who boldly address the much-needed issues that are currently boiling in our society. Sure, I've heard it said many times, "Choose your battles wisely," but the main point here is that we were not called to become stagnant pew warmers, but to become kingdom warriors who put on God's full armor and are always prepared for spiritual warfare.

To be *transformed* is a personal choice in which we allow the Word of God to continually renew our heart and mind, but to be *conformed* is a choice in which we allow current cultural doctrine to shape our heart and mind. And if the body of Christ is being conformed, we will become blind to the little furry cubs that have infiltrated and continue to infiltrate our local churches, but if we allow the Holy Spirit to transform our hearts and minds on a regular basis, we will be able to discern Satan's deception and expose these cuddly cub lions.

*"Transformation of our heart and mind is a continuous process, not a one-time occurrence."*

## THE OPOSSUM SYNDROME

Why is it that we can boldly quote passages like "Turn the other cheek," "Love your neighbor," "Forgive and it shall be forgiven you," or our personal favorite, "Love the sinner," but we become blind to what is going on around us? This is what I refer to as *The Opossum Syndrome*. This is how the syndrome appears. We read the Bible, pray, fast, and shout the loudest during church, but when it comes to addressing or confronting the critical issues that are attacking, degrading, or suppressing our Christian values and biblical beliefs, we tend to remain silent as if nothing is happening. Why is this so?

Here are some interesting facts about opossums. They have large razor-sharp teeth and may hiss or growl, but when threatened, frightened, or in danger, they faint or play dead on the ground. This is why I chose this amusing but sobering example to illustrate how Christian people can easily hiss and growl at one another, especially when it comes to theology, biblical truths, or what worship should be, but when it comes to dealing with or confronting vital issues pertaining to our faith or the sanctity of God's Word, they simply play dead. Perhaps it's because these people are already spiritually dead. Just a thought to ponder on!

> *"The true essence of discipleship is not handing out spiritual pajamas but equipping every born-again believer with the armor of God."*

## WE NEED MORE NINJA SHEEP

Who exactly are ninja sheep? I'm glad you inquired! When I first started following Dr. Lance Wallnau, he coined the phrase "ninja sheep." In their workplaces, academia, society, and other settings, ninja sheep are Christians in disguise. In other words, these people are born-again believers who do not present or portray themselves as religious zealots who act like Jehovah's Witnesses and irritate everyone.

Ninja sheep Christians are people who understand their kingdom purpose, identity, and the sphere of influence that God has given them. And as they function in that specific sphere, they release God's glory and majesty, as those around them begin to be changed, if not transformed. Again, these ninja sheep Christians are self-assured and courageous in their faith in front of others. And as long as you and I operate as these types of ninja sheep, the lions of this world will be unable to devour our faith or the living Word of God that resides in our spirit man.

> *"Be bold as a lion, because the Lion of Judah lives within you."*

# CHAPTER 13
# CHRISTIANS OR CRITICS?

Christians or critics? Is that meant to be a trick question? No! But I'm glad you asked. You see, we're all critics to some extent because we have a fallen human nature, and it's difficult not to be critical of something or someone. That is not the case when your criticism is a hobby for you, and because you do it so frequently, you almost don't notice how your heart has a critical spirit.

Here are a few things to think about when it comes to those who spit out criticism like sunflower seeds:

- Those who criticize frequently have accomplished nothing in their lives but will gladly criticize those who have.
- Those who criticize are usually suffering from a personal identity crisis and have yet to discover their God-given identity and purpose on this earth.
- Those who criticize are frequently motivated by jealousy.
- Those who criticize are usually insecure and full of fear.
- Those who criticize are known to harbor resentment and unforgiveness.

- Those who criticize may be doing so blindly, as a result of their own brokenness and emptiness.

The truth is that many people who criticize others for their specific accomplishments or achievements have done nothing themselves, and they believe they are now qualified to criticize those who have. This was especially evident among the Pharisees and Scribes, who constantly mocked and ridiculed Jesus. This type of heart attitude has been mentioned numerous times in the Bible, including by Jesus Himself. The Pharisees were the Bible's harshest critics, and this critical spirit lives on in millions of Christians around the world. And as you read this chapter, the honest question you and I must ask ourselves is, "Am I a Christian or a critic?"

> *"Making others greater than you are the heart and essence of biblical discipleship."*

## CRITICISM IS NOT INSTRUCTION

In the book of Proverbs, we read, "Whoever loves instruction loves knowledge, but he who hates correction *is* stupid."[1] The amazing thing here is that there are so many critics or those who believe that criticism is their spiritual gift and that when they criticize their fellow brother or sister in Christ, they believe they are providing them with sound instructions or sound correction. Furthermore, over the years, I've discovered that these same types of people have an inner conviction that the Lord is using them as a tool to help bring the body of Christ or their fellow Christian back into biblical spiritual alignment.

I'm so grateful that Jesus can serve as an example to us all in all aspects of life, especially when it comes to criticism. With all of the miracles, supernatural wonders, and other amazing things that Jesus did on earth like no other human being, He was savagely criticized. It's one thing that no one can see a supernatural miracle, but it's quite another to personally witness a supernatural occurrence and then mock the person who demonstrated it. This was exactly what happened to Jesus on a regular basis.

A critical spirit is more than just a character flaw; it is a spiritual disease that, if not addressed, will gradually erode your spirit man and even your faith. My brother and sister in the Lord, instead of criticizing your fellow Christian, I challenge you to position your heart and spirit man to help others with the help of the Holy Spirit. Individuals with a critical spirit abound in our world and society as a whole. Let God's children not correlate with such people.

> *"Religious discipleship presents God's Word to you as a rulebook, but kingdom discipleship reveals God's Word to you as your guidebook."*

## ME, MYSELF, AND I

Critics typically have a three-fold identity: Me, Myself, and I. It's all about me in life! I'm in love with myself! And I have the attitude that I am the center of the universe. This kind of heart attitude has been weakening the entire body of Christ. And if we truly want to be Christ's disciples, we must remember that Jesus did not come into this world to live for Himself, to please Himself, or to force others to serve Him simply because He was the Son of the living God.

Again, Jesus found ways to teach His disciples about true servanthood, as demonstrated by the washing of the disciples' feet. This act was so incredible that even Peter became uneasy when he saw the Son of God kneeling to wash his feet. This same principle, both spiritually and physically, needs to be practiced more in the body of Christ. And the more we turn our attention away from ourselves and toward our neighbors, the easier it will be to serve others, and the less we will notice in others.

> *"The day you genuinely desire to become a disciple of Christ is the day you begin to focus on others rather than yourself."*

## MOM AND DAD, ARE YOU SOWING WHEAT OR TARES?

Having three children has put my wife and me on a fast track. So far, our parenting journey has been adventurous, exciting, and intriguing. And, once again, I'd like to emphasize the important role that parents play in their children's lives by asking, "Mom and Dad, are you sowing wheat or tares into your child's life?" This question is meant to test you and me to see if we are operating with a critical or a God-given spirit.

As parents, we may be unaware that our homes, dinner tables, and car rides are all forms of classrooms in which our children are the primary students. And what we talk about, who we talk about, and how we talk about others will become a curriculum from which your child will draw knowledge and answers, whether it's good or bad. I've seen my own parents say harsh things about other people, including church leaders, without realizing that their children were sitting right next to them, soaking up every negative word. And I'm also very guilty in this regard, as my mouth has said things around my own children that have planted wrongful seeds in their innocent hearts.

Some of you may not find this to be an eye-opener or a revelation so far, but I'd like to take it a step further. One thing we as parents often overlook or dismiss is that you are the most influential person in your child's life. As a result, what your child hears from your lips has a much greater impact on their heart, sub-conscience, and spirit man. In other words, if mom or dad is driving home from church and complaining about how bad the sermon was, or why churches should not allow dancing or clapping, or why the music is too loud, or the worship songs are too contemporary, or why the pastor is not spiritual enough, or why the church allows so many secular things, those little innocent ears are quietly consuming every word that you are speaking, and those words become seeds that sow in their spiritually immature hearts and in due time they will sprout forth unpleasant fruit.

Please allow me to emphasize this point once more. In a nutshell, no matter how anointed or impactful the service was, it will all be rendered useless and irrelevant because you went on a legalistic rant about how disappointed you are with what happened during today's service. What am I trying to say here? Your negative and toxic religious words have more power than you realize, Mom and Dad, and many people wonder why my son or daughter grew up hating God or despising Christianity. Hello! It only took a twenty-minute car ride back home to spiritually drain your child's heart and mind as you endlessly criticized your church, pastor, or sermon. So, are you a Christian, or are you just a typical critic who is constantly dissatisfied with anything that does not align with your spiritual comfort zone?

May I kingly remind you that if you are a seasoned Christian, your local church is no longer about you, but about those who do not know the Lord or about the lost sheep, as Jesus once powerfully stated, that He leaves the ninety-nine sheep behind to go look for the one lost sheep.[2] And I believe that this is where many Christian folks got the church concept wrong, and why many become disgruntled, dissatisfied, or criticize the pastor or church leaders. They would have a much more spiritually mature heart attitude if they truly understood that church is not about them.

> *"The younger generation is eagerly awaiting the emergence of spiritual fathers and mothers."*

# CHAPTER 14
# I DON'T BELIEVE IN THAT STUFF

When you don't understand something, what do you usually do? You ask questions or seek clarification! What do you usually do when you are perplexed or hear something confusing? Again, you ask questions or seek clarification! And what would you normally do if someone made a daring or outrageous statement? Well, you try to go back to the original source to find out what was said and whether or not it is true. Right?

For whatever reason, many so-called Christians today resemble a deer caught in the headlights and on the verge of being run down by a truck. For instance, you claim that there is a heaven and a hell and that those who do not accept Jesus Christ as their Lord and Savior will be cast into hell. And their reply is, "I don't believe there is a hell." You say that demons exist and that they torment or possess people, and they respond, "I don't believe in demons." All of the preceding applies to those who identify as Christians. So, what is the source of such vehement opposition to such undeniable facts? Let's take a look at this chapter to find out more.

## GOD IS LOVE...PERIOD!

Why would a loving God, who sacrificed His only Son, Jesus, on the cross, condemn someone to hell? That may be a very intelligent question, but it lacks substance and credibility. Why? Well, the Bible says, if you read it carefully, "The Lord is not slack concerning *His* promise, as some count slackness, but is longsuffering toward us, not willing that any should perish but that all should come to repentance."[1] Or how about the Bible's most famous verse: "For God so loved the world that He gave His only begotten Son, that whoever believes in Him should not perish but have everlasting life."[2] Interesting! According to both scriptures, God does not want anyone to perish.

Nothing can ever change the fact that God is love, but He is also faithful to His Word. And the Bible is full of passages that state unequivocally that God despises sin, lawlessness, immorality, and idolatry, to name a few. And, while the Bible is full of love, hope, forgiveness, and redemption, it is also full of warnings for those who choose to live a life of sin and disobedience to God's law. And as God's children, we must rightly balance God's love in accordance with what the Bible has already outlined, without attempting to erase the other side of His love, which manifests itself in the form of discipline and warnings. This is what true discipleship entails!

## I DON'T BELIEVE IN THAT STUFF

Angels, demons, the devil, hell, eternal damnation, or eternal torment in the lake of fire aren't everyone's spiritual cup of tea. And, yes, I'm referring to Christians! When it comes to the integrity of God's Word, we can either position our hearts and spirits to accept and believe in the entire Bible, or we can pick and choose what sounds more appealing.

Again, hearing about an all-loving, all-merciful, and all-forgiving God makes everyone happy, but we will mock others as righteous zealots when they quote passages like, "Now the works of the flesh are evident, which are: adultery, fornication, uncleanness, lewdness, idolatry, sorcery, hatred, contentions, jealousies, outbursts of wrath, selfish ambitions, dissensions, heresies, envy, murders, drunkenness, revelries, and the like; of which I tell you beforehand, just as I told you in time past, that those who practice such things will not inherit the kingdom of God."[3] Or, "Do you not know that the unrighteous will not inherit the kingdom of God? Do not be deceived. Neither fornicators, nor idolaters, nor adulterers, nor homosexuals, nor sodomites, nor thieves, nor covetous, nor drunkards, nor revilers, nor extortioners will inherit the kingdom of God."[4]

Whether you believe it or not, the truth will not go away. The Word of God is God's Word. Whether you believe in the whole Word or bits and pieces, the Word of God has no less power or authenticity. For example, j ump out of the plane without a parachute and exclaim, "I don't believe in gravity!" Gravity will simply smile and wait for you to splatter all over the ground. Alternatively, you could say, "I no longer want to put gasoline in my car, but will replace it with water because it is cheaper." When your car won't start, you'll be confronted with harsh reality once more. In other words, simply choosing not to believe in something does not make it magically disappear. The Bible is not an exception to this rule.

> *"Ignorance or denial will never justify or defend anyone when they stand before the all-powerful and just judge."*

# CHAPTER 15
# REVIVAL OR REFORMATION?

For a time, especially in my early years, I was a strong proponent of talking about and preaching about revival. There's nothing wrong with that, but my perspective has shifted in recent years, and this has a lot to do with maturity, as well as certain men and women of God I've been following and listening to. So, what exactly happened?

Dr. Lance Wallnau, who I find very intriguing and who I also regard as a powerful prophetic voice, and a watchman on the wall who is sounding a loud trumpet by telling the body of Christ to wake up and get out of your religious slumber. He frequently says, "Churches do not need a revival, but they need a reformation." Why? He then continues to elaborate this thought a bit further, "Because revival touches the individual, while reformation touches institutions like academia, the media, the government, the marketplace, and the arts & entertainment."

Let's take a closer look at Dr. Lance Wallnau's profound statement. So, why is revival primarily aimed at individuals rather than the entire nation? First, we must ensure that our heart, spirit man, and mindset have been revived so that we can have the mind of Christ and become yielded vessels in God's hands. Only then will we be in a position to bring reformation and transformation to our community, society, and world.

Furthermore, when we have the mindset that we need to pray and fast for revival for our local community or our nation, we begin to overlook the fact that if we as the local church are not spiritually revived or in the right spiritual alignment, all of the above will not occur in the way that we desire. Does this imply that God will disregard our prayers and fasting? No, but what we are doing is backward.

I once heard the late pastor David Wilkerson say in one of his sermons that the primary reason many churches in New York City became empty a few months after September 11th was that those churches were not spiritually prepared for the great influx of souls. Thousands upon thousands of people flooded every church in New York City in fear of what happened on that dreadful day, but many churches were not spiritually revived for such a harvest.

In my book, *Can I See Your ID?,* I outlined the significance and distinction between my identity *in* Christ and my identity *through* Christ! When I receive my redemption, salvation, forgiveness, and legal rights to call myself a child of God, that is when I find my identity in Christ. But discovering my identity through Christ is when I discover my purpose, calling, and assignment on this earth. So, when it comes to *revival*, it's the same as me discovering who I am in Christ, and when that happens, everything within me is revived. But *reformation* is the same as discovering my purpose and assignment on this earth, and as I begin to operate in my gifting and potential, I begin to bring kingdom reformation into my family, my workplace, my neighborhood, my business, academia, social media, and society as a whole. And in this chapter, I want to challenge you, my friend, not to get caught up in all of the catchy spiritual sound bites that we may hear at conferences or from prominent Christian leaders, but rather to first position ourselves to be revived by the Holy Spirit and the living Word of God, and then to position ourselves as yielded vessels to bring reformation in the area of our kingdom purpose and calling.

> *"Personal revival will align your heart to know your identity in Christ, whereas reformation will position you to know your identity through Christ as He begins to use you for His greater purpose on this earth."*

## THE JONAH SYNDROME

What exactly is the *Johan Syndrome*? I'm glad you asked! The story of Prophet Jonah is unique, somewhat humorous, and extremely pathetic all at the same time. Jonah had a kingdom calling as a prophet, and the Lord gave him a direct assignment to preach to the city of Nineveh. When Jonah heard the Lord's command, he packed his belongings and sailed in the opposite direction of his assignment. Then, while the prophet Jonah is sound asleep, a violent storm breaks out, and the ship is on the verge of collapsing. Jonah eventually admits to his disobedience before the rest of the shipmates and then is thrown into the sea, swallowed up by a large fish, and eventually ends up in Nineveh.

You'd think Jonah had learned his lesson. Right? Certainly not! He preaches a doomsday message to the citizens of Nineveh and then sits on a hill to enjoy the heavenly firestorm that he believes God will pour down on Nineveh and burn it to the ground. That never happened, and Jonah became enraged at God. This is what I refer to as *The Jonah Syndrome.*

This syndrome is very visible in the body of Christ, but not in the way you might think. This syndrome has nothing to do with whether Christians want to or dislike evangelizing to their neighbors or coworkers; rather, it has to do with the fact that we are unconcerned about our city or town, state, or nation. Jonah was tasked with preaching to a city of more than 120,000[1] people, and his mission was not to do street evangelism but to bring a kingdom influence to the entire city.

Again, revival is dealt with on a personal level, where the Holy Spirit is reviving an individual's inner spirit man, whereas reformation is meant to influence a city, or a whole state, or a region, or your local community, and our heavenly Father is strategically positioning every child of God all over the world as types of Jonah's who will function and operate in their kingdom assignment at their local schools, at work, in their local communities, and wherever the heavenly Father is sending them. And as we all position our inner hearts to be used by the Lord, we will begin to see a great outpouring of God's power and move like never before, as long as we do not have the same wrong heart attitude as Jonah. And Apostle Peter shares the heart of God towards all living souls when he said, "The Lord is not slack concerning *His* promise, as some count slackness, but is longsuffering toward us, not willing that any should perish but that all should come to repentance."[2]

# CHAPTER 16
# I DID NOT SIGN UP FOR THIS

As God's children, we sometimes forget to read the fine print, or is that just the original blueprint, which is God's Word? When you made the decision to give your life to Jesus and become a follower of Christ, you signed up for an exciting life full of blessings, prosperity, health, favor, divine connections, and plenty of trials and suffering. What! What trials and tribulations?

The Bible is known as the Good News that speaks the truth, and those who choose to receive and live by this truth will face much demonic opposition, criticism, betrayals, backstabbing, and numerous trials. Are you serious? I did not sign up for this!  And in this specific chapter, I'll give you a biblical overview of what it means to be a true disciple of Jesus and what you and I should expect.

> *"True disciples of Jesus will be tested in times of crisis because adversity fosters spiritual growth and maturity."*

# THE PROOF IS IN THE PUDDING

The Bible is full of good examples of biblical characters we admire and look up to who faced many difficulties, trials, and suffering. Let's take a quick look around at some of them:

- **David** was continually persecuted by King Saul.
- **Daniel** was thrown into the den of lions.
- **Shadrach**, **Meshach**, and **Abed-Nego** were thrown into the fiery furnace.
- Baby **Moses'** life was in jeopardy as his generation of males was slaughtered.
- **Apostle Paul** was stoned to death, shipwrecked, and beaten numerous times.
- **Stephen** was martyred.
- **John the Baptist** had his head chopped off.
- **Jesus** was endlessly criticized and eventually crucified.

As much as it encourages us to read about these heroes of faith, we have a tendency to believe that these tribulations are limited to those described in the Bible. This could not be further from the truth. Anyone who sincerely desires to be a true disciple of Christ will face trials, hardships, persecution, and even martyrdom. And, as the saying goes, "the proof is in the pudding," which means that the Bible has already demonstrated to us that God's children are not immune to adversity and various challenges.

## GODS HOLY FIRE WILL TEST EVERYTHING

Your theology, beliefs, ideology, doctrines, personal foundation, and works will all be put to the test by God's holy and righteous fire. The Word of God declares, "For no other foundation can anyone lay than that which is laid, which is Jesus Christ. Now if anyone builds on this foundation *with* gold, silver, precious stones, wood, hay, straw, each one's work will become clear; for the Day will declare it, because it will be revealed by fire; and the fire will test each one's work, of what sort it is. If anyone's work which he has built on *it* endures, he will receive a reward. If anyone's work is burned, he will suffer loss; but he himself will be saved, yet so as through fire."[1]

You see, your theology is only as good and credible as it is after it has been tested by the Lord's fire. Similarly, the Lord will put to the test your man-made traditions, denominational doctrines, and church ideologies. The question that we must all seriously consider is how much of our own work will be burned away simply because God was not the source of it, or because it was full of flesh?

The word "fire" in the Bible usually has two meanings. The first refers to God's wrath and punishment, while the second to cleansing or purification. For example, we sing a lot of songs with lyrics like "Send your fire Lord." Or, "Allow your fire to come." Or "We need more of your fire." And when this fire comes, it will serve its purpose for cleansing someone's heart and purifying their life, or as a fire of judgment. The choice is always ours.



## I DID NOT SIGN UP FOR THIS

When we gave our hearts to our Savior, Lord Jesus, on that special day in our personal lives, it was truly a transformational and historical moment. Having said that, many new converts, including myself, failed to read the fine print. That fine print outlined not only all of the blessings we will receive in our walk with the Lord, but also a slew of difficulties, trials, tribulations, backstabbing, betrayal, and even persecutions. Wait a second! I did not sign up for this!

The Word of God is full of such fine prints as we read in the gospel of Luke, "But I say to you who hear: Love your enemies, do good to those who hate you, bless those who curse you, and pray for those who spitefully use you."[2] Difficulties, trials, and various demonic attacks on our lives are all part of our Christian faith and walk with the Lord.

Being a true follower of Jesus has many benefits and blessings, but it also has many difficulties, as Jesus reminded His disciples when He said, "Remember the word that I said to you, 'A servant is not greater than his master.' If they persecuted Me, they will also persecute you."[3] Again, it appears that we, as God's children, have created the delusion that serving and following in the footsteps of Jesus is simple. Yes, from one point of view, but when we closely examine the gospels, we can clearly see that Jesus gives us many warnings, and if we want to be a true follower of Christ, we must be prepared for much discomfort, opposition, hatred, and even persecution.

Here are a few crazy thoughts for you to consider in relation to Christianity or those who consider themselves to be followers of Jesus:

- It is normal for the world to reject you.
- People of the world will look at you differently.
- You will not fit in with the worldly lifestyle or culture.
- Your faith and convictions will make others uncomfortable.
- You will lose certain friends, connections or even business opportunities because of your biblical beliefs.
- Your kingdom light, righteous standing and holy living will make others uncomfortable.

Some Christians have turned the true gospel message into a religion that teaches that God is all-loving, all-forgiving, and all-merciful no matter what. That is true, but we cannot limit God's attributes to the positive without also teaching and preaching that God is also a judge, and He is not blind or ignorant to those who choose to live a double life. And, yes, I was speaking of Christians! And when you chose to accept Jesus as your Lord and Savior, you automatically signed up for a completely different way of life that must be significantly different from the worldly way of life.

> *"Various trials, criticism, suffering, or persecution are only tools used to strengthen your faith and bring you closer to your heavenly Father."*

# CHAPTER 17
# THE RESUME OF TRUE DISCIPLESHIP

Anyone who fills out a job application is expected to submit a resume and, at times, a personal cover letter. A resume is typically a document that details your work history, achievements, and academic credentials. These resumes are used by those who do the hiring or vetting to quickly filter through to determine whether the applicant meets their basic requirements or not.

This principle holds true for discipleship as well! In what way? As we read the Bible, we come across many people who demonstrated great commitment, dedication, faithfulness, and obedience to the Lord, as well as many who did the opposite. And all of their actions were recorded in God's Word, which we are reading about today. So, in a way, reading about specific individuals and who they were and what they did is similar to reading their personal life resume.

Fear of not being qualified for a specific job is a common stress that many new applicants experience when filling out a job application. I personally went through a period in my life when my income was drastically reduced due to the loss of some work contracts. This resulted in me frantically filling out over 400 applications and spending hundreds of hours looking for work over the course of two years. And one of my biggest challenges while filling out these applications was that I lacked the necessary academic credentials but had more than enough work experience, and more than 90 percent of my applications were rejected as a result. Or I would not pass the interview process.

In this chapter, I'd like to take a different approach by listing some biblical characters and their personal resumes, as well as pointing out how all of them lacked the necessary credentials, experience, or qualifications, but the Lord still used them powerfully:

1. **Apostle Peter's Resume**
   - He denied Christ three times.
   - Allowed Satan to speak through him.
   - Had a big mouth.
   - Cut off a high priest's servant's ear.
2. **Samson's Resume**
   - Was a womanizer.
   - Broke his covenant with God.
   - Was made blind and became a prisoner.
3. **Apostle Paul's (Saul's) Resume**
   - Murdered and imprisoned the followers of Christ.
4. **Jonah's Resume**
   - Disobeyed a direct command from God.
   - Was thrown overboard and had one whale of a ride.
5. **Moses' Resume**
   - Killed an Egyptian

6. **Jacob's Resume**
   - Was a professional liar.
7. **Apostle Thomas' Resume**
   - Was always full of doubts.
8. **King David's Resume**
   - Lustfully took another man's wife, got her pregnant, and eventually killed her husband.
9. **Noah's Resume**
   - Got drunk with wine and laid naked in his tent.
10. **Rahab's Resume**
    - Was a professional prostitute.
11. **King Solomon's Resume**
    - Had way too many girlfriends.
12. **Abraham and Sarah's Resume**
    - They both had doubts about God's promise being true and authentic, so they gave birth to Ishmael.

So, what's your lame reason for refusing to let the Lord use you? If any of us has the audacity to believe that there is at least one thing that rightfully qualifies us to be used by God, we are making a grave error. Why? As he stated in the book of Romans, Apostle Paul provides one of the best answers. "For everyone has sinned; we all fall short of God's glorious standard."[1] It is because of our sinful nature that we are all disqualified. But thanks to Jesus' blood, redemption, and reconciliation, we can now boldly approach our heavenly Father through His Son Jesus and obtain a brand-new kingdom resume.

## WHAT IS THE RESUME OF TRUE DISCIPLESHIP?

True discipleship always entails growth. Growth is also a sign of spiritual health. Staying spiritually healthy will put your heart, mind, and spirit man in a position to be a vital blessing in the lives of others, which will automatically bless your life. However, spiritual growth in discipleship occurs on various levels.

I'm grateful that the Bible is always rich in practical examples that we can take and apply to our spiritual growth, and John's first epistle gives us a unique outline of what spiritual growth looks like at different levels:

*I write to you, **little children**,*
*Because your sins are forgiven you for His name's sake.*
*I write to you, **fathers**,*
*Because you have known Him who is from the beginning.*
*I write to you, **young men**,*
*Because you have overcome the wicked one.*
*I write to you, **little children**,*
*Because you have known the Father.*
*I have written to you, **fathers**,*
*Because you have known Him who is from the beginning.*
*I have written to you, **young men**,*

*Because you are strong, and the word of God abides in you,*
*And you have overcome the wicked one.*[2]

The passage above identified three groups: "little children," "young men," and "fathers." All three represent different stages of spiritual development. And John uses the opportunity to explain each group's spiritual maturity level. And if we earnestly desire to have the resume of a true disciple of Christ, we must always apply biblical principles and concepts to our personal lives and spiritual growth. This growth process will take time, but it is critical for every child of God to go through because it will allow our heavenly Father to use us as kingdom tools for His greater purpose.

> *"True kingdom disciples never graduate from the school of discipleship; rather, they are continual students until the day they die."*

# CHAPTER 18

# THE WATCHMAN ON THE WALL

The term Watchman on the wall has been used in a variety of contexts throughout Christianity, but I want to focus on how it is used in the context of discipleship. When we read the Bible, we see that God used the implication of the watchman to refer to the spiritual leaders of the time. In addition, we should understand the historical application and functionality of a watchman.

Watchmen were individuals, most often of the military variety, who stood on the city walls and kept watch for any potential enemy or danger that might approach their city. These guards were stationed on the walls 24 hours a day, seven days a week. If one of these watchmen fell asleep, the punishment was swift and unapologetic execution. Why? Because a single watchman could have jeopardized the city's security and well-being. This was also a powerful message to the rest of the watchmen to remain vigilant at all times.

One critical issue that is sweeping through the body of Christ is that too many watchmen are falling spiritually asleep or are distracted by something else. The watchmen are those who hold a specific position of authority or influence or who bear a specific responsibility. Church leaders, parents, teachers, political figures, business owners, and other influential people are among them. And, yes, I am speaking specifically to born-again believers, not the world's influencers.

And just as in the time of prophet Ezekiel, God is speaking the same words to the body of Christ:

*Again the word of the LORD came to me, saying, "Son of man, speak to the children of your people, and say to them: 'When I bring the sword upon a land, and the people of the land take a man from their territory and make him their watchman, when he sees the sword coming upon the land, if he blows the trumpet and warns the people, then whoever hears the sound of the trumpet and does not take warning, if the sword comes and takes him away, his blood shall be on his own head. He heard the sound of the trumpet, but did not take warning; his blood shall be upon himself. But he who takes warning will save his life. But if the watchman sees the sword coming and does not blow the trumpet, and the people are not warned, and the sword comes and takes any person from among them, he is taken away in his iniquity; but his blood I will require at the watchman's hand.'*[1]

In this chapter, I will discuss the importance of why every born-again person is being positioned as a watchman on the wall and why, more than ever, we as God's children must stand guard over our spiritual life, our family, our marriage, and our local church.

## BLOWING THE TRUMPET OR PLAYING A LOVELY SONG?

When the watchman saw an enemy approaching the city or any other trouble, he blew the trumpet. The watchman couldn't care less if it was noon or two o'clock in the morning. The watchman is also unafraid of disturbing someone's sleep, waking up someone's baby, agitating the king, or even hindering someone's romantic evening; he is a watchman, and his sole responsibility is to protect the civilians who live within the city walls.

The watchman does not operate or function based on feelings, emotions, or even political correctness; rather, they operate and function based on the duty and responsibility that has been bestowed upon them. This divine principle also holds true for pastors, church leaders, and parents. If any of the above are swayed by their congregation, or a fellow believer, or their child, just to avoid hurting their feelings or possibly losing a church member, then your purpose and duty as a watchman have been compromised, and the above warning passage in Ezekiel states that their blood will be on your hands.

As a pastor, a church leader, or as a parent, are you blowing the trumpet of awareness or are you just playing the trumpet as a sweet melody? And even God revealed to the prophet Ezekiel some powerful insights about how the Israelites of his time received the Lord's Word from his lips:

*"As for you, son of man, the children of your people are talking about you beside the walls and in the doors of the houses; and they speak to one another, everyone saying to his brother, 'Please come and hear what the word is that comes from the LORD.' So they come to you as people do, they sit before you as My people, and they hear your words, but they do not do them; for with their mouth they show much love, but their hearts pursue their own gain. Indeed you are to them as a very lovely song of one who has a pleasant voice and can play well on an instrument; for they hear your words, but they do not do them."[2]*

This was not a compliment uttered by God through the mouth of Ezekiel, and in the same way, we must position our heart and spirit man in the same way as Ezekiel to continually speak the truth, whether others accept it or not. And that truth must be heard as a trumpet of the Lord, not as a lovely song in the ears of those who are dying. This is one of the kingdom assignments for being a watchman on the wall.

> *"The trumpet of the Lord is meant to awaken you and me from our spiritual slumber so that we can be watchful in these last days."*

# THE RELIGION OF INCLUSIVENESS, TOLERANCE, AND WOKENESS

Our world is filled with numerous and diverse religions, with the Protestant community alone having over forty thousand different denominations,[3] and people in India worshiping over three hundred million different gods and goddesses.[4] This may not come as a surprise to you, but in recent years, our culture has incorporated new religions known as:

- Religion of *Equality*
- Religion of *Inclusiveness*
- Religion of *Counterculture*
- Religion of *Expression*
- Religion of *Feminism*
- Religion of *Independence*
- Religion of *Wokeness*
- Religion of *Tolerance*
- Religion of *BLM*
- Religion of *Political Correctness*
- Religion of *Cancel Culture*

So, why did I choose to label all of the preceding as religions? They are, after all! The dictionary defines "religion" as a specific fundamental set of beliefs, doctrines, and practices generally agreed upon by a number of persons or sects.[5] Very intriguing! So, if someone has a strong fundamental belief, convictions, or ideology, they are motivated to defend and advocate for what they believe in.

Right? Absolutely, and we are seeing, more than ever before, that the above ideologies, which are similar to religious doctrines, are specifically capturing the hearts and minds of the younger generation. Why the younger generation?

Throughout history, the younger generation has always served as stepping stones and building blocks for the world to come. Just as children carry on their family's name and legacy, or we have many businesses that have been passed down from generation to generation, the same is true for any local church, where the younger generation is "the church of tomorrow."

With that said, history has a dark side where the younger generation was groomed for a destructive purpose, as was so visible during Hitler's era, who captivated the hearts and minds of his nation's children and youth. I go into great detail about it in one of my previous books in a chapter titled *Hitler's Deadly Vision*. The key point to remember is that Hitler captured the hearts of the younger generation when they were still children, and when he unleashed his lethal vision years later, these same youth were now his army captains, police chiefs, and political leaders.

Religion, or religious indoctrination, functions in a similar manner. Whatever belief, ideology, or doctrine you continually instill in the heart and mind of an individual will bear fruit in due time. And if religions of equality, tolerance, or wokeness continue to be pushed down the minds of the younger generation, our society as a whole will soon reap the deadly consequences of such religions.

Some of you reading this may be perplexed as to why I chose to include these things in this book. And the answer is very clear, as we are witnessing these same religions creeping through the doors of our local churches, with the younger generation being the most vulnerable to this current phenomenon. And it is for this reason that I have chosen to sound the alarm as a watchman so that my fellow brothers and sisters in Christ can be alerted to the demonic strategy that is raging against the body of Christ.

> *"Man's fallen nature has redefined and will continue to obstruct God's original plan for mankind. However, His purpose and truth will always be intact."*

## THE GOATS WILL BE SEPARATED FROM THE SHEEP

When we read Matthew 25:32-46 carefully, we grasp the idea that Jesus is the true shepherd who will separate and divide the sheep from the goats. And it's easy for someone to assume that the sheep are Christians, and the goats are atheists. However, this is not the case. The sheep and goats were both from the same flock, just as wheat and tares grew together in the same field until harvest time when they were separated. The key verse, in this case, is, "Then they will answer Him, saying, 'Lord, when did we see You hungry or thirsty or a stranger or naked or sick or in prison, and did not minister to You? And these will go away into everlasting punishment, but the righteous into eternal life."[6]

The keyword here is that the goats on the left side responded, "Lord," indicating that they were aware of the Lord but did not know who He was. In other words, our churches are full of goat Christians who meet once a week, but their hearts and spirit man are far from the Lord. And, with so many current world events, we are witnessing and will continue to witness, a separation of the sheep and the goats. Why? Because Jesus, the true Shepherd, has a kingdom mandate for America and the entire world, and He will not tolerate so-called goat Christians who have trampled the sanctuary and the Word of God.

For the sake of clarity, who would fall into the goat category? Here's a quick rundown:

- These people have become social justice warriors, but they have also become politically correct in order not to offend others with the truth of God's Word.
- These people have stopped drinking from the living waters and have started drinking the world's Kool-Aid.
- These people express their outrage by saying, "This is my body," while also supporting abortion.
- These people accept the toxic ideologies of our current culture while challenging and dismissing the fundamental principles of God's Word.
- These people stand side by side in support of those who lead immoral lives, shouting, "The Bible is an outdated book."

- These people became entrapped in politics and political parties, ignoring the King and His Kingdom's mandate.
- These people vote with their heads and their personal headstrong ideologies, rather than with their inner convictions, which are founded on biblical truths, morality, and Godly principles.
- These people incite rivalries in their local church.
- These people are frequently the driving forces behind church splits and separations.
- These people would gossip about their pastor or church leader behind their pastor's or church leader's back.

If we believe that all of the preceding applies only to the secular world, we would be mistaken; the preceding refers to millions of so-called Christian people all over the world. This is not a mystery or a surprise; simply open your social media and see what some of your fellow Christians are discussing or passionately supporting. Or simply observe some of the Christian folks in your local church.

> *"The sheep listen to and submit to the shepherd's (Jesus') voice, whereas the goats willfully rebel against the Lord's Word."*

## THE WATCHMEN AND WATCHWOMEN MUST STAY SPIRITUALLY AWAKE

As I mentioned at the beginning of this chapter, if a watchman fell asleep at their post, their punishment was immediate execution, as that particular watchman could have jeopardized the entire city, and thus this could be used as a valuable lesson to others. Staying awake was a top priority or ultimate responsibility that every watchman had to observe, and this principle is also true for our modern-day watchmen and watchwomen that our Lord has placed in every local church. And we would be tragically mistaken to believe that these people are limited to the well-known pastors and ministries that we are all familiar with.

It is easy to become obsessed with the idea that the body of Christ has specific assigned individuals such as pastors, prophets, apostles, prominent Christian leaders, or those who are very influential around the world who have a specific calling to be these watchmen and watchwomen. This could not be further from the truth. Every one of us is a watchman or a watchwoman, and we all need to have internal discernment about what is going on around us and what the Holy Spirit is showing us.

Staying awake was one of each watchman's primary directives, and this also applies to us as God's children staying spiritually awake, especially in these dark days. And even Jesus encountered this problem during His most critical hour when He was battling all of hell in the Garden of Gethsemane and found His disciples sleeping: "Then He came to His disciples and found them sleeping, and said to Peter, "What! Could you not watch and with Me one hour?[7] The keyword was, "watch." And after Jesus rebuked Peter, He left again to pray.

You'd think Peter and Jesus' disciples would have learned something here, but they didn't. Jesus returns again and says, "Are you still sleeping and resting?"[8] This same rebuke is being issued today by the Holy Spirit, who is telling us to "be watchful," to "stay spiritually awake." To be watchful means to be on guard, to be vigilant, to be aware of the spiritual season we are currently in, and to be alert to the devil's tactics and deception. And as I close this chapter, I'd like to encourage you, my fellow kingdom ambassador, to rise up at your post as a watchman or a watchwoman to be ready to sound the trumpet because no one knows the day or the hour of His coming, which is closer than we may think.

> *"Always be on guard and vigilant, because the enemy of your soul is always looking for an opportunity to strike you down."*

# CHAPTER 19
# WHERE IS MY BELT?

When I was a kid, one of my most fearful moments was when my parents were looking for the belt. I knew right then and there that my butt cheeks were going to hurt for the next few hours. But, decades later, I believe I turned out alright and that my parents' physical discipline did not traumatize me. But what if our heavenly Father says, "Where is My belt?" Similarly, we all know that our spiritual butt cheeks will experience His love and mercy on a whole new level.

As we journey through this breathtaking chapter together, you will need to take a deep breath because the heat is about to increase to a new level. And my sole purpose in this chapter is to emphasize that God's love is not blind or foolish, and that persecution of the body of Christ is on the rise. Furthermore, I will address the sensitive issue of who Christian snowflakes are, as well as the fact that the body of Christ is currently experiencing a spiritual pandemic like never before.

> *"The Lord's discipline will always make you uncomfortable, so get used to it."*

# GOD'S LOVE IS NEITHER BLIND NOR NAÏVE

Love was the force that brought two hearts together in holy matrimony. It was love that brought the husband and wife together in intimacy, which was later evident by the birth of a child. Furthermore, it is the mother's love for her infant that will rouse her from her sleep to attend to the needs of the crying baby. And it is love that motivates us all to invest our time, money, and energy, even if it means sacrificing our health, for the sake of those we love. As a result, love is a powerful force.

This was the same love that poured out of heaven from our heavenly Father's heart in the form of His Son Jesus, who died for you and me so that we could have eternal fellowship with our Creator. And this same love continues to flow inexhaustibly through this earth, particularly towards God's children. That being said, human love can be reversed in an instant, as those who once declared their love for one another during their wedding ceremony are now attempting to kill one another in hatred and bitterness. Or the parents who foolishly exclaim, "I hate you; I wish you had never been born." However, this is not the case with our heavenly Father.

When God, our Father, is upset or even angry with His children, He does not send legions of angels to destroy us or to punish us with various diseases, as some Christians believe. No, He pulls out His belt in the form of His living Word and tells us that He is not pleased with us. Furthermore, the fact that God has not responded with righteous judgment or discipline does not imply that He is foolishly blind to how His children are misbehaving or how the body of Christ is embracing immorality. He is full of love, mercy, and patience, but He can only tolerate sin and lawlessness for so long before He pulls out His belt.

***"The love of the Father is sweet to your soul, bitter to your flesh, and satisfying to your spirit man."***

## READY OR NOT PERSECUTION IS COMING

Many people are hoping for a revival and the next great awakening, but before either of those things can happen, America needs to be cleansed. And as Christians, especially in the free nation of America, we have a tendency to overlook the concept of persecution. However, as we read the Bible, we come across numerous passages that discuss persecution. And even Jesus emphasized this uncomfortable subject when He said, "If the world hates you, you know that it hated Me before it hated you."[1] And, "Remember the word that I said to you, 'A servant is not greater than his master.' If they persecuted Me, they will also persecute you."[2]

I honestly cannot say that I am more courageous or have more faith than my fellow brothers and sisters in the Lord who live in hostile countries that kill Christians for sport, but I do come from a background of persecution and religious oppression as I was born in the former Soviet Union, and I have already shared a portion of my testimony in previous chapters. And, while I wholeheartedly enjoy my freedom and liberty in the free nation of America, I don't want to become complacent in the knowledge that this liberty will not last forever. Hopefully, I've piqued your interest!

None of us can be fully prepared or ready for persecution, but we should not be blind to the fact that it is on the horizon and that we are already experiencing some of its symptoms. Returning to Jesus' words, "If they persecuted Me, they will also persecute you." He did not say, "they might," but "they will." Sorry for flattening your spiritual tires in this chapter, but when we are fully aware and knowledgeable of the entire truth of God's Word and grasp on to every word of Christ, we will not be left hopeless, but rather encouraged to continue doing the Lord's business until He comes.

> *"Whenever people resist, mock, or oppose what you believe in and stand for, it is a sign of how strong and healthy your faith is."*

## SNOWFLAKE CHRISTIANS

The term *snowflake* was recently introduced into the lexicon to describe someone who is unable to deal with opposing viewpoints, which eventually agitates and incites hatred within that individual and often hurts their emotional and intellectual feelings. So, with that in mind, how would this term be applied to Christians?

You've probably noticed that I don't reserve specific words or terminologies because my sole goal is to capture your heart, mind, and spirit man in order to express my inner passion for the body of Christ and my fellow Christian man. And the reason I purposefully chose to include this issue in this book is that I have witnessed, and continue to witness, Christian people who melt away in their anger, rage, and hatred towards their fellow brother or sister in Christ simply because they hold opposing views.

Similarly, I witnessed this so evidently during the pandemic year of 2020 and the chaotic year of 2021. As I previously stated, I am very active on social media and with what is going on in the political arena. And as I began to address some of my concerns, political assessments, or what was going on in the body of Christ in relation to the Word of God, I received a lot of pushbacks from my fellow Christians, particularly from certain pastors and church leaders. Even some of them unfollowed me, while others began to repost critical posts on their social media platforms, which I knew were in response to what I had posted earlier.

It is beneficial when we can agreeably disagree because it promotes healthy dialogue. But it's a completely different story when you've touched a spiritual nerve in someone who chooses not to engage in that healthy dialogue with you, but instead goes to their social media followers and begins their spiritual rant complaining about how "unloving" or "hateful" some of their Christian connections are. As this is nothing new, the sensitivity level of Christian people has skyrocketed, and instead of addressing the critical questions or concerns about the health of the body of Christ and the influence of the local church, we moan and groan and complain about what other Christian people are saying, which bothers such people because they are like snowflake Christians. Furthermore, rather than dividing the body of Christ because you choose to be a baby Christian, it is these types of sensitive subjects that need to unite us more than ever before.

> *"Your faith and personal relationship with Jesus will be put to the test on a regular basis. It is entirely up to you whether you will remain strong or crumble."*

## A SPIRITUAL PANDEMIC

The year 2020 was not what most people around the world expected. Years ago, social media and numerous influential Christians declared and stated that the year 2020 would be visionary. It will herald the start of something new and extravagant. To everyone's surprise and dismay, the year 2020 will go down in history as a year that transformed the entire world and placed us in a different way of life in which the entire world had to readjust their thinking and readjust the way we did business, attend schools, become more health-conscious, and the list goes on.

The year of the pandemic will also go down in church history as the year when the body of Christ experienced its own spiritual pandemic in such a dramatic way that we are still seeing and will continue to see the aftereffects in the coming years. In March of 2020, my family and I were attending a phenomenal church with approximately 20,000 members,[3] and we felt both blessed and spoiled to be a part of a local church with a strong spiritual shepherd and a powerful vision. As a result, all churches in America were forced to close their doors to slow the spread of COVID. As a result, every local church was forced to completely restructure its church services and programs, and everyone switched to the online church model.

This appeared to be a good thing at first, as many people began to use the social media platform to stay in touch with their church members and fellow believers. However, what was intended to be a temporary thing has become the norm for many believers who chose to forego in-person attendance and instead continue to watch their Sunday service in their pajamas or even in their underwear.

So, what was the spiritual pandemic that began to occur in the body of Christ? Instead of releasing their inner faith, God's children and church leaders began to operate more in fear. Christian believers began to put their faith in scientists rather than the Savior. They began to consume every word spoken by the CDC rather than every word from the KJV. Pastors and church leaders began to rely more on what politicians and local governments said, rather than inclining their spiritual ears to hear from the heavenly Father.

As destructive and deadly as COVID was, the spiritual pandemic in the body of Christ has killed off many believers and forced the closure of many churches. When our church reopened its doors again, about a month later, the pastor was troubled in his heart when he stated that our attendance was around forty percent, at that time. Some may argue that people stayed at home out of fear of contracting COVID from another person. This may appear justifiable at first, but people simply chose to stay at home, and many eventually dropped out because they had grown accustomed to not attending their local church.

Again, the spiritual pandemic began in the body of Christ when we began to operate more from our flesh and trusted man more than the Son of Man. According to God's Word, "For God has not given us a spirit of fear, but of power and of love and of a sound mind."[4] Instead of positioning the local church and God's children as lighthouses during the pandemic storm, we placed our light under the basket of fear. While the world was filled with fear and uncertainty, the local church joined the world and began to share in the same fear, dismissing Jesus' powerful saying, "You are the light of the world. A city that is set on a hill cannot be hidden. Nor do they light a lamp and put it under a basket, but on a lampstand, and it gives light to all *who are* in the house. Let your light so shine before men, that they may see your good works and glorify your Father in heaven."[5]

The reality check questions that we must all ask are: Did our light shine before others who were in fearful darkness? Was our local church positioned like a city on a hill, where others could seek refuge? And, for the most part, the answer was no. It may be tempting for some of you to think that I'm judging you or your church leadership for the decisions they had to make, but that would be a complete disservice to the purpose of this entire book, which is to stir up the hearts and spirit man of my fellow brothers and sisters in Christ to be proactive rather than pathetically reactive.

I sincerely believe that what the body of Christ went through in 2020 and 2021 was a kind of test, in which we miserably failed, but what hope we all have through the undeserving grace of our heavenly Father, who does not easily give up on His children, that we will eventually recognize our weaknesses, repent, and become the light to this dying world.

> *"The spiritual health of the body of Christ will be determined by how much it submits to God's perfect will."*

## THE SOCIAL MEDIA CHURCH

As I previously stated, following the recent pandemic of 2020, the local church and how we did church has drastically changed. And the idea of having or doing church on social media platforms has erupted like a volcano. Some in a positive way, and many in a negative way. In what way? Going to church appears to have taken on a whole new meaning, where you can simply sit in your underwear or pajamas and attend your local church via your TV or Smartphone. Why not? We are able to do so because of technological advances.

So, here's something to think about: Reading your Bible or a book on a digital device is not the same as actually touching the pages. Even psychologists and researchers have observed that when a person uses their fingers to touch and feel the pages of a book, their brain and senses send a completely different message to their brain. A frozen microwaved meal, for example, will never taste the same as a home-cooked meal. Furthermore, you will never treat a rental car the same way you would treat your own car or your own home in comparison to a rental.

All of the above speaks loud and clear with the same truths that it is not the same as attending your local church in person or doing church online. And no justifiable reason will justify anyone's excuse for why online church service is more beneficial or acceptable than in-person church service. And, as the author of Hebrews put it bluntly, "And let us consider [thoughtfully] how we may encourage one another to love and to do good deeds, not forsaking our meeting together [as believers for worship and instruction], as is the habit of some, but encouraging *one another*; and all the more [faithfully] as you see the day [of Christ's return] approaching."[6]

The preceding passage was not a recommendation, but rather a gentle warning, in which the AMP Bible translation uses the word *habit* to state that some believers have a bad habit of missing worship services. This is now a clear picture of what is going on in the body of Christ, where some Christians consider it normal to skip out on regular worship services by remaining home at their own comfort.

And, as much as I believe in using every available social media platform and tool to preach the kingdom gospel and disciple others, we should never replace in-person fellowship, and no pandemic, no government laws, or political oppression should ever prevent God's children from expanding His kingdom and fellowshipping with one another.

> *"Do not exchange your fellowship and worship with others for the sake of fleshly comfort, as Esau exchanged his birthright over a bowl of soup."*

## THE FATHERS LOVE IN A FORM OF A BELT

Growing up, there was one Bible verse that I heard my parents say frequently and even experienced on a large scale, "He who spares the rod hates his son, but he who loves him disciplines him promptly."[7] This Bible verse was drilled into both my ears and my butt cheeks. And, by God's grace, I survived. And now that I am a parent of three, I have learned that discipline is a healthy and normal practice in any family, and the same divine principle holds true for our heavenly Father.

When a child is disciplined by their parent, they may believe that their mother or father does not love them, which is far from the truth. This same ideology is shared by God's children who despise and even hate the Lord's discipline, but if we truly desire to be God's children, we must adhere to the original script as stated by the author of Hebrews. "For whom the Lord loves He chastens, and scourges every son whom He receives."[8] Why is this truth so vital for every child of God to grasp? The Hebrews author continues, "If you endure chastening, God deals with you as with sons; for what son is there whom a father does not chasten?"[9]

Again, we understand the significance of God disciplining us because we are His children, but as we read the next verse, we encounter a cautionary warning, "But if you are without chastening, of which all have become partakers, then you are illegitimate."[10] Wow, this is a bold statement in which we must all honestly evaluate our hearts and make a decisive decision as to whether we consider ourselves to be God's son or daughter. However, the author of Hebrews continues to elaborate on this powerful thought. "Furthermore, we have had human fathers who corrected *us*, and we paid *them* respect. Shall we not much more readily be in subjection to the Father of spirits and life? For they indeed for a few days chastened *us* as seemed *best* to them, but He for *our* profit, that *we* may be partakers of His holiness. Now no chastening seems to be joyful for the present, but painful; nevertheless, afterward it yields the peaceable fruit of righteousness to those who have been trained by it."[11]

Just in these few verses, we are introduced to the genuine love of our heavenly Father. Here are a few key points to keep in mind:

- The Father disciplines those He loves and accepts into His family.

- God the Father treats us as if we were His children.
- Because He disciplines us, we are reassured that we are His legitimate children.
- Our heavenly Father disciplines us for our own good and benefit.
- We become partakers of His holiness when we are disciplined.
- Our heavenly Father's discipline will produce the fruit of righteousness in us.

Even though our heavenly Father's love is expressed in the form of a belt, it gives us hope that we are loved by Him and that we are being treated as His children, rather than as world outsiders who do not know or receive Him. And even as we are being chastised by Him, we must examine our relationship with the Lord and re-evaluate our spiritual condition.

> *"Because our heavenly Father genuinely loves His children, we should not be angry with Him when He expresses His love, mercy, and grace in the form of a belt."*

# CHAPTER 20
# RAISING INFLUENTIAL DISCIPLES

Raising influential disciples is not a new or trendy concept in today's church culture, but it can be traced back to what Jesus did with His twelve disciples. The word *influential* means: persuasive, strong, inspiring, important, dominion, and leadership.[1] And while the Bible is full of love, mercy, grace, forgiveness, and hope, we should not forget that it is also full of people who did radical and influential things. Let's look at a few of them in more detail:

- **Jesus** flipped over the tables of the moneychangers and constantly did miracles on the Sabbath day!
- **Apostle Peter** walked on water!
- **David** killed a massive giant with a slingshot!
- **Mary** preserved her sexual purity and gave birth to the Messiah!
- **Daniel** intimidated a pack of hungry lions!
- **Josheb-Basshebeth** killed eight hundred men at one time!
- **Abishai** killed three hundred men with his spear!
- **Esther** risked her life as she boldly went before the king!
- **Samson** killed a lion with his own bare hands!

- **Moses** fasted for forty days without food or water!
- **Jonathan** was constantly putting his life in danger to protect his friend David.
- **Ruth** separated herself from her own people and accepted Naomi's God and people wholeheartedly!
- **Matthew** gave up his lucrative tax business to follow Jesus.
- **Peter** was the only one who walked on water.

As the body of Christ, we must begin to raise radical and influential disciples rather than pitiful churchgoers! We need to train one another for spiritual warfare, not church games. We need to be honest with one another, saying things like, "you will have to endure hardships," or "your faith will be tested through adversity, criticism, and various oppositions." And in this chapter, I wanted to address a few key points by challenging you to consider whether you are more focused on manmade traditions or the kingdom mandate. Understanding the significance of paying the price for being a true disciple of Christ. And why it is critical to developing kingdom leaders.

> *"Making converts is the same as becoming a parent after having a child, but making disciples is the same as becoming a father and a mother. Anyone can have a child, but not everyone becomes a father or mother."*

# MANMADE TRADITIONS vs KINGDOM INFLUENCE

Throughout the history of Christianity, particularly during the time of Jesus and throughout the Old Testament, we encounter a plethora of man-made traditions with little or no biblical support or connotation. However, these manmade traditions played an important role in shaping the hearts and minds of millions of believers. And these manmade traditions continue to inundate the body of Christ to this day.

Should we be concerned about these manmade traditions, or should we simply disregard them because there is nothing new under the sun? Some traditions can be ignored, but many have and continue to bind many born-again believers with religious legalism, which in the process blinds their hearts and mind from understanding the simplicity of God's Word.

So, why do I bring up an age-old issue or symptom that was, is, and will continue to afflict the body of Christ? Because it's a serious spiritual problem that, in some cases, is spreading like cancer in just about every local church. I won't bore you with my personal life journey as a young born-again believer; you can read about it in my book, *Generation Gap: Raising the Next Generation of Leaders.* And remember that our heavenly Father has entrusted us with His kingdom keys, not with manmade doctrines or theological ideologies. And it is for this reason that we must function as influential kingdom ambassadors, growing in the authenticity of God's Word and building God's kingdom on earth with what He has already equipped us with, rather than with manmade traditions.



## SALVATION IS FREE, BUT BEING A DISCIPLE OF JESUS WILL COST YOU

Jesus taught and shared much kingdom knowledge and wisdom with His inner circle disciples, and it would have been very tempting for them to become very relaxed and comfortable with Jesus, as walking side by side with the Son of God was a rare privilege. But Jesus, in His infinite wisdom, knew He had to keep His message real, and at one point He told His disciples, "If anyone desires to come after Me, let Him deny himself, and take up his cross, and follow Me."[2] The two keywords in the preceding verse are, "deny yourself." And the word *deny* means to forsake, to sacrifice, or to say no to yourself. This does define exactly what Jesus did when He walked upon this earth.

One of the most difficult challenges for many born-again believers or those who are still new in their faith is to not be relieved that salvation was given for free, even though it cost Jesus His life, because our carnal human nature will never cherish those things that were given to us for free, and the same principle applies to salvation. We were spared the agony of the cross. We did not have to give up our personal lives. And it is because of this that many people fail to fully appreciate the free gift of salvation, which costs us nothing.

Therefore we must all bear the cost of being a Christ-follower. Just as we cherish something more because we paid for it with our own money, so too, as we pay the cost of being a follower of Jesus, we will have a greater value and appreciation for being his disciple. This is an important truth that all of God's children must understand.

So, what exactly does it mean to be a true disciple of Jesus Christ? Here are a few fundamental requirements:

1. Forsake your worldly lifestyle and friends to follow Christ wholeheartedly.
2. Believe and testify that the Bible is the truth and not a collection of opinions.
3. To be in a covenant with Christ rather than a contract.
4. You must be prepared to sign on as a soldier, ready for battle, rather than as a fan joining a social club.
5. Be prepared to become salt to the world rather than sugar.
6. Be willing to change by laying down your fleshly desires at the foot of the cross.
7. Allowing your heart, mind, and thoughts to be renewed in accordance with the Holy Word on a regular basis.
8. Be ready to roll up your sleeves and get to work building God's kingdom on earth.

*"The growth of your church or ministry will be measured not in numbers, but in how many lives will be changed and transformed."*

## GROOMING KINGDOM LEADERS

I was originally born in the former Soviet Union, and I recall two profound moments in my early childhood life when I was around eight years old, before immigrating as a refugee to the United States of America. One incident occurred when I was in first grade, and in communist Russia, every school once a week had a *lineika* (Soviet patriotic roll-call).[3] This *lineika* was just another piece of Communist propaganda designed to brainwash students. Its sole purpose was to indoctrinate the younger generation with the Communist Party's ideology and why Communism was the way of life.

During this *lineika*, the principal and teachers would congratulate specific students on their accomplishments and devotion to the Communistic directive by tying a red scarf in the shape of a tie around their neck. Others would be given a pin depicting Vladimir Lenin or the red Communist star. During this *lineika*, the principal would also speak about the outcasts and traitors of Mother Russia, and the perpetrators were usually Christians. And, following the principal's vehement speech, she would order everyone who was a Christian to come forward so that the entire school could see who these traitors to Mother Russia were. And of course, I, along with my siblings and fellow Christians would step forward.

As we did, the principal and teachers would mock us in front of the entire school, calling us a disgrace to Mother Russia, and then they would purposefully place a Communist pin on our school uniform as a sign of mockery to our Christian faith. Throughout the school year, this was done about once a week.

Another instance occurred when I was hospitalized in a children's hospital for about a month due to a virus infection, and during one of the children's daily naps, I was pulled out of my bed and placed in front of the doctors and nurses. And while they were eating their lunch, they would make fun of me, mock me, and ask me a variety of questions about why I chose to believe in this foolish religion known as Christianity. As far as I can recall, I didn't say anything to them.

Surprisingly, I don't recall feeling scared on either occasion. Why? My parents must have done an excellent job of instilling the fundamental principles of our Christian faith in me and all of my siblings. And my parents repeatedly warned us that we would be mocked, laughed at, and possibly beaten as a result of our faith. They would also encourage us by pointing out that Jesus had to go through similar ordeals.

My parents did an excellent job of instilling in me the necessary kingdom principles that enabled me to withstand the harshness of Communism as an eight-year-old. And it is because of this that my heart and spirit man is strong to this day. No, I'm not perfect, but I have a strong spiritual foundation. With that said, God forbid you tell a fellow believer today that their way of life is sinful or unholy, and they will melt like snow with rage and bitterness. Or, if you tell a fellow believer that they need to be bold about their faith and inner convictions, and they will respond, "But I don't want to hurt anyone's feelings." Or, God forbid, you start teaching the true essence of discipleship, which means you'll be persecuted, hated, despised, attacked, or even killed for your faith. No way! You'd be called a religious bigot.

My main point here is that we need to groom kingdom leaders who will become radical and transformational disciples who will not be intimidated by the world's fiery furnaces, lion dens, or crucifixions. Furthermore, let us look at some of the defining moments in the lives of biblical characters that established them as kingdom leaders:

- **Daniels's** defining moment occurred in the lion's den.
- **David's** defining moment was when he faced Goliath.
- **Shadrach**, **Meshach**, and **Abednego's** defining moment were in the furnace.
- **Esther's** defining moment took place when she entered before the king without an invitation.
- **Apostle Paul's (Saul's)** defining moment occurred on the road to Damascus.
- **Rahab's** defining moment took shape when she hid the two spies from her own people.
- **Abraham's** defining moment painfully occurred when he was about to sacrifice his son Isaac.

- **Apostle Peter's** defining moment was when he denied Jesus three times.
- **Joseph's** defining moment was shaped through being sold into slavery by his brothers, falsely accused, and while in prison he still served with his gift.

These are only a few of the many examples found in the Bible. We must embrace life's trials and tribulations because it is in these critical moments that you are often defined as who you are, what kingdom potential you have, and what you are called to do on this earth. And whether we want to accept this divine principle or not, we often discover who we are and what potential resides within us during our most difficult times.

You see, the success or the future of your local church or your ministry will be determined and measured by whether you are grooming and discipling kingdom leaders. This is precisely what Jesus was doing with His twelve disciples. And to groom kingdom leaders is not suggesting church folks to regularly attend Sunday services, or having a daily prayer life, or memorize Bible verses, but to help each and every individual to become fully rooted and grounded in their identity in Christ, and helping them to discover their purpose and potential, as they will become valuable tools in the hands of the almighty God.

## ARE YOU A KINGDOM LEADER OR AN AVERAGE CHURCHGOER?

What does it mean to be a kingdom leader? When it comes to leadership, some people have a misconception. Some believe that "leaders are born," while others believe that "leadership is not for everyone," and still others believe that "you must be called by God to be a leader." All of the above is untrue, because God has given us dominion over the earth, and He also calls us to be the head, not the tail.[4] Furthermore, kingdom leaders drastically standout from average churchgoers. Let's take a look at some of my personal *Stanverbs*:

- A ***Kingdom Leader*** is a lion who behaves like the king of the jungle, whereas an ***Average Churchgoer*** is a house cat who behaves like the king of the couch.
- A ***Kingdom Leader*** is like a team player, whereas an ***Average Churchgoer*** is just a player on the team.
- A ***Kingdom Leader*** is the first to say, "I'm sorry," whereas the ***Average Churchgoer*** is the first to demand an apology.

- A ***Kingdom Leader*** never stops moving forward, whereas the ***Average Churchgoer*** always searches for the nearest rest area.
- A ***Kingdom Leader*** will carry their name into history books, whereas an ***Average Churchgoer*** will have their name etched on a tombstone.
- A ***Kingdom Leader*** influences others, whereas an ***Average Churchgoer*** is influenced by others.

Hopefully, the above comparison did not offend you, as I attempted to illustrate a point in a humorous manner. And the point is that you have every right to be an average churchgoer who loves the Lord, tithes, attends church on a regular basis, reads the Bible, and prays daily, but that is not the true description of a disciple of Jesus Christ.

If I may be transparent and vulnerable in front of you, my fellow brother and sister in the Lord, I honestly do not believe that anyone who chooses to be an average churchgoer, at least as I have described earlier, will not find true satisfaction in their faith and personal walk with the Lord. And the reason for this is that our heavenly Father has placed kingdom potential within every living human being, waiting to be discovered and released. And no matter how hard you try to suppress the Holy Spirit's internal promptings; they will never go away.

> *"Giving your life to Jesus makes you a disciple of His but discovering your identity in Christ makes you a kingdom leader."*

# Chapter 21
# KINGDOM DISCIPLESHIP

Kingdom discipleship is not some kind of a fancy or creative slogan, but rather a proactive kingdom mandate. As born-again Christians, we must always have the heart attitude of being proactive. According to the Thesaurus, the word "proactive" means: *to be aggressive, can-do attitude, dedicated, energetic, full of enthusiasm, to be excited, to be fired up, to be passionate, and to take charge.*[1]

So, for you and me to be proactive kingdom disciples, we must roll up our sleeves and be fully dedicated to the kingdom mandate, as our inner heart is all fire up for the Lord, and we take charge and move forward with much passion and excitement in fulfilling His will on this earth. And in this final chapter of the book, I'd like to pose a question to you: what is your local church producing? While at the same time reminded all of us that as seasoned believers it is no longer about us, but about those who are lost or those who are still immature in their faith. And finally, to stir up your heart and spirit man with much excitement that we all should focus on *doing the Lord's business until He comes.*

## WHAT IS YOUR LOCAL CHURCH PRODUCING?

I wholeheartedly believe that every local church was called to fulfill a specific kingdom assignment in their geographical location, which often happens to be their town or the city where the church is located. On the surface, this may appear to be common sense, but I'd like to pose a thought-provoking question, "What is your local church producing?" As an example:

An **apple** tree will reproduce more apples!
A **lion** will reproduce a lion cub!
**Baptists** produce more Baptists!
**Catholics** produce more Catholics!
**Charismatics** produce more Charismatics!
**Methodists** produce more Methodists!
**Pentecostals** produce more Pentecostals!
**Religion** will reproduce religious churchgoers!
**Jesus** produced disciples!

When we read the original text of God's Word, we were told to go into all the world and make disciples. Right? Or were we tasked with going into the entire world and make more Baptists, Catholics, Charismatics, Methodists, and Pentecostals? Furthermore, consider that legalism produces more legalists, religion produces more religious zealots, man-made traditions produce average churchgoers, but disciples produce more disciples.

Again, what is my local church producing? And as a friendly reminder, the lost, the brokenhearted, the hurting, and the outcasts are not looking for a religion or manmade doctrines or theological experts, but they are in desperate need of those who can help them to reconnect with their Creator. This is a powerful takeaway, that we as the body of Christ should stay focused on the original kingdom assignment that Jesus has left for us all. And one more vital thought to consider is that the success or the future of any local church will be determined and measured by whether or not they are raising and discipling the next generation.

> *"The ultimate goal of true discipleship is to produce kingdom disciples, not to maintain churchgoers."*

## IT'S NOT ABOUT YOU!

When I started writing this book in 2019, my family was a proud member of Free Chapel, which was led spiritually by pastor Jentezen Franklin, who is widely regarded as one of the greatest and most influential kingdom leaders in the body of Christ today. My family received many blessings, much Word, much wisdom, and plenty of spiritual spankings during our seven years under the powerful visionary leadership of Free Chapel. Pastor Jentezen, during his sermons, would occasionally include the phrase "It's not about you!" And this phrase was frequently used to emphasize the idea that if you are a seasoned Christian, the church is no longer about you, but about those who do not know Christ or are still new in their faith.

This same phrase began to speak loudly and clearly into my and my wife's inner spirit man, and at the end of 2020, we both began to re-evaluate our walk with the Lord as the Holy Spirit nudged us to get out of our comfort zone, and at the beginning of 2021, we both made a radical decision that we thought we would never make as we transitioned out of Free Chapel, and joined a new church family, New Life Church of Atlanta. And as wise King Salomon once said, "A man's heart plans his way, but the Lord directs His steps."[2] In our hearts, there was a strong desire to begin releasing our inner kingdom purpose and potential, and our heavenly Father simply began to direct us in the polar opposite direction of what we both expected.

And in no time, the senior pastor and other church leaders at New Life Church recognized our potential and gifts and challenged us without hesitation to begin releasing and imparting them into the local church family. As I write this, my family has been a part of NLC for about six months, and I have personally experienced many blessings and inner fulfillment as a result of releasing my inner kingdom potential into the local church, which is different from constantly receiving and not giving away. And the author of Hebrews' words rang out loud and clear when he said, "For though by this time you ought to be teachers, you need *someone* to teach you again the first principles of the oracles of God; and you have come to need milk and not solid food. For everyone who partakes *only* of milk *is* unskilled in the word of righteousness, for he is a babe. But solid food belongs to those who are of full age, *that is*, those who by reason of use have their senses exercised to discern both good and evil."[3]

These verses speak of spiritual maturity, and we must all reach this point when it is no longer about us and how good we feel at church, but about us laying aside our selfishness, laying aside our spiritual milk bottles, rolling up our sleeves, and getting busy doing the Lord's business until He returns. And, as much as Free Chapel blessed my family, our spiritual graduation has occurred, and the time has come for us to function in the kingdom assignment that our heavenly Father has bestowed upon us.

> *"The moment when you discover and understand your kingdom purpose on earth, will become the day when you will focus off yourself and will begin to focus on others."*

## DOING THE LORD'S BUSINESS UNTIL HE COMES

As I conclude this book, I'd like to revisit Jesus' words to his parents: And He said to them, "Why did you seek Me? Did you not know that I must be about My Father's business?"[4] One significant takeaway is that Jesus was still a teenager when He made this profound statement, and it would be another seventeen years before He would officially step into His purpose and calling as the Messiah. This is something that all of God's children must understand in our spirit man.

Doing the Lord's business will shift your focus away from yourself and toward others. And as we do so, we position ourselves to remain proactive until He comes. Doing the Lord's business will challenge God's children to be kingdom-minded so that they do not become enslaved by their fleshly desires. And doing the Lord's business will allow our heavenly Father to carry out His perfect plan on earth as He originally planned through His living Word.

And we are introduced to another power kingdom of heaven parable that Jesus said in Matthew chapter twenty-five, where He illustrates about a wealthy businessman (type of God the Father) who gave his servants talents (money), but one of his servants was lazy and buried his one talent. When this man returned from his trip, he inquired of his servants as to what they had done with his money. And when this one lazy servant told his master that he had buried his talent, his master became enraged and took away his one talent, and said, "To those who use well what they are given, even more will be given, and they will have an abundance. But from those who do nothing, even what little they have will be taken away. Now throw this useless servant into outer darkness, where there will be weeping and gnashing of teeth."[5]

The parable above is a great example of how each of us has been given unique gifts, talents, and potential that we must use to glorify God on this earth. However, if we choose to be lazy, just like that servant, we will reap the same bitter fruit. And being a part of our heavenly Father's business is a tremendous honor and opportunity. With that said, my fellow brother and sister in the Lord, I implore you not to become weary, distracted, or discouraged by everything that is happening in our world, but to yield your heart and body to the leading of the Holy Spirit, who will equip you with the necessary kingdom tools, guide you in the direction that you need to go, and reveal to you what role and purpose you play in God's greater business plan.

Yes, Jesus is returning for His Bride, and while no one knows the day or hour, it should only encourage and motivate us to continue doing His kingdom business, knowing that at any moment Jesus is coming back with great eagerness and overwhelming joy, knowing that His Bride is waiting for Him.

And as you and I continue to be faithful until the end, we must constantly remind ourselves and others that we must keep our inner fire for the Lord burning, because smoke has never attracted anyone. Let us come together as one body, in one spirit, in one unity, to doing the Lord's business, not knowing the day or the hour of His return but having hope that our eternal redemption is near. And allow the words of James to comfort you: "You also be patient. Establish your hearts, for the coming of the Lord is at hand."[6] And in the Book or Revelation, John concludes with these final words that complete the whole Bible as he declares, *He who testifies to these things says, "Surely I am coming quickly." Amen. Even so, come, Lord Jesus!*[7]

> **"True kingdom discipleship is to make disciples who will eventually become greater than you."**

# NOTES

Introduction
1.   Luke 2:49

**Chapter 1 – Doing The Lord's Business Until He Comes**
1.   https://green.brainyquote.com/quotes/tony_evans_914446?src=t_part-time
2.   Luke 9:23
3.   2 Timothy 2:3
4.   Romans 12:2

**Chapter 2 – Are We babysitting or Making Disciples**
1.   Heb 5:12-14 (NLT)
2.   1 Thessalonians 1:5
3.   Luke 14:26-27 (CEV)
4.   Revelation 3:16
5.   1 Cor 13:11 (NIV)

**Chapter 4 – Political Correctness vs The Truth**
1.   Luke 12:56
2.   Philippians 2:9-11
3.   https://dictionary.cambridge.org/us/dictionary/english/politically-correct
4.   John 8:31-32
5.   John 18:37b-38

**Chapter 5 – A Pharisee or a Child of God?**
1.   Matt 23:13-16, 25, 27
2.   John 13:34-35

**Chapter 6 – Where Is My Reward?**
1.   Matt 9:37b
2.   Matt 6:3-4

**Chapter 8 – Un-Brainwashing The Brainwashed**
1.   Luke 11:52 (NLT)

**Chapter 9 – Please Stick To The Original Script**

1.   Matt 28:19a
2.   2Tim 4:3-4

**Chapter 10 – Politicians, Theologians, or Ambassadors?**
1.   Luke 12:8-9
2.   Matt 25:33
3.   2 Corinthians 5:20a

**Chapter 11 – 95/5 Principle**
1.   Eph 6:20a (NLT)
2.   1 Corinthians 12:4-6
3.   1 Corinthians 12:28-31

**Chapter 12 – The Cat Has Grown Into A Lion**
1.   1 Peter 5:8 (NLT)
2.   Romans 12:2

**Chapter 13 – Critics or Christians?**
1.   Prov 12:1
2.   Matthew 18:12-13

**Chapter 14 – I Don't Believe In That Stuff**
1.   2 Peter 3:9
2.   John 3:16
3.   Galatians 5:19-21
4.   1 Corinthians 6:9-10

**Chapter 15 – Revival or Reformation?**
1.   Jonah 4:11
2.   2 Peter 3:9

**Chapter 16 – I Did Not Sign Up For This**
1.   1 Corinthians 3:11-15
2.   Luke 6:27-28
3.   John 15:20a

**Chapter 17 – The Resume of True Discipleship**
1.   Romans 3:23
2.   1 John 2:12-14

**Chapter 18 – The Watchman On The Wall**
1.   Ezekiel 33:1-6
2.   Ezekiel 33:30-32
3.   https://www.dictionary.com/browse/religion?s=t

4. https://www.livescience.co
   m/christianity-
   denominations.html
5. https://apnews.com/article/
   24bfb9b360e30268ce87764
   b6f65bb72
6. Matt 25:44,46
7. Matthew 26:40
8. Matthew 26:45a

**Chapter 19 – Where Is My Belt?**
1. John 15:18
2. John 15:20a
3. https://www.charismanews.
   com/us/76796-jentezen-
   franklin-we-need-to-be-
   honest-about-the-elephant-
   in-the-room
4. 2Tim 1:7
5. Matt 5:14-16
6. Hebrews 10:24-25 (AMP)
7. Prov 13:24
8. Heb 12:6
9. Heb 12:7
10. Heb 12:8
11. Heb 12:9-11

**Chapter 20 – Raising Transformational Disciples**
1. https://www.thesaurus.com
   /browse/influential
2. Matthew 16:24
3. https://histclo.com/youth/y
   outh/org/pio/nat/rus/act/ca
   mp/pr-acampa.htm
4. Deuteronomy 28:13

**Chapter 21 – Kingdom Discipleship**
1. https://www.thesaurus.com
   /browse/proactive
2. Proverbs 16:9
3. Hebrews 5:12-14
4. Luke 2:49
5. Matthew 25:14-15 (NLT)
6. James 5:8
7. Revelation 22:20

# ABOUT THE AUTHOR

Stan is an entrepreneur, author, life coach, and a kingdom influencer. He is passionate in helping others to discover and understand their identity in Christ through coaching, mentoring, and discipleship.

**StanBelyshev.com**

# OTHER BOOKS BY THE AUTHOR

## Rated R
*A Biblical Perspective On Dating, Relationships, Marriage, And Sexual Purity*

# The 52 Laws of Kingdom Leadership

*Discovering And Understanding True Biblical Leadership*

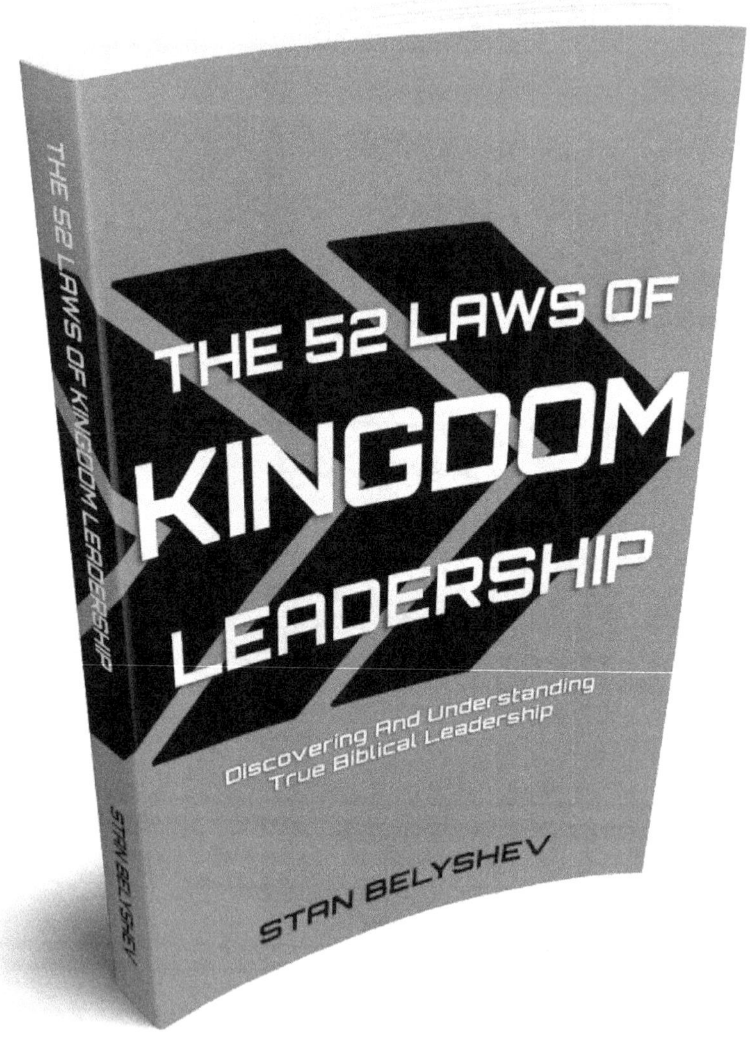

# Can I See Your ID?
## *Discovering And Understanding Your Purpose and Identity*

*Know your identity in Christ!*
*Know your identity through Christ!*

# MANHOOD
## *Restoring Biblical Manhood*

# God IS Good
## *No Matter What God Is A Good God*

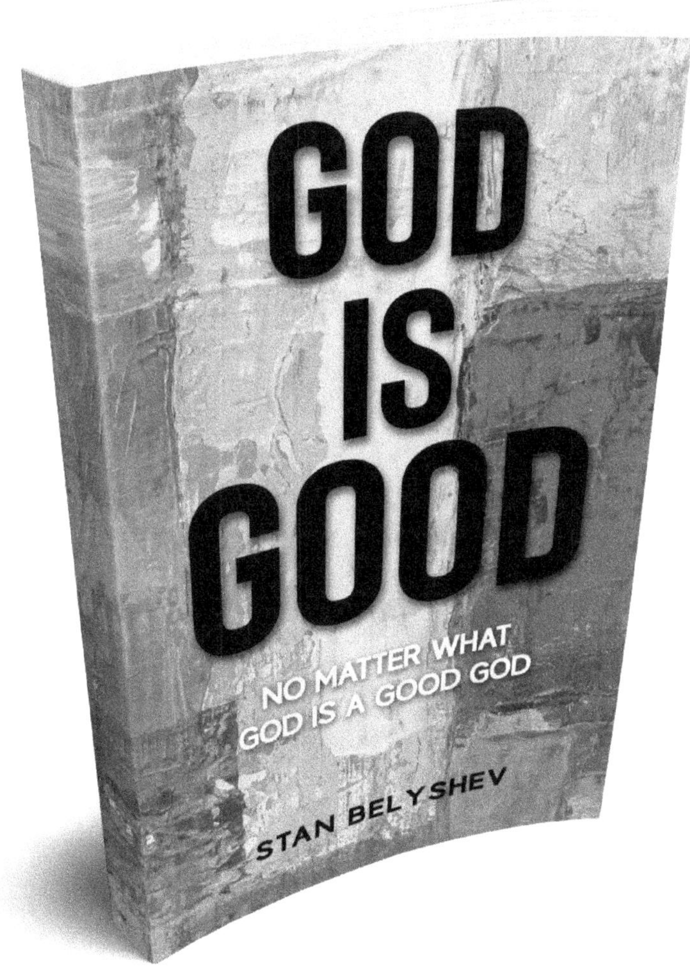

*Is God A Good God?*

# When Life Is Full of It
## *An Antidote For Your Mind*

*"Our world is already full of it, so please do not be a contributor."*

# Generation Gap
### *Raising The Next Generation of Leaders*

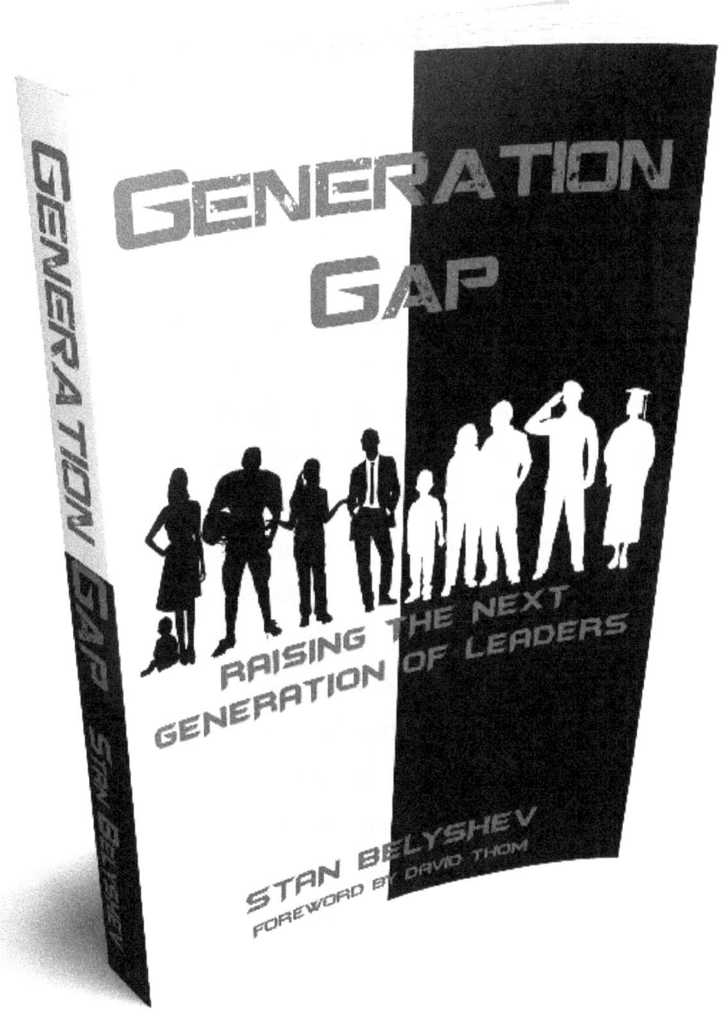

# SOCIAL MEDIA

https://www.youtube.com/@stanbelyshev

https://twitter.com/StanBelyshev